TEACHINGS

OF

SHĀH WALĪYULLĀH

TEACHINGS OF SHĀH WALĪYULLĀH

of

DELHI

By

G. N. JALBANI

Formerly Professor and Head of the Department of Arabic
University of Sind, Hyderabad

KITAB BHAVAN
New Delhi-110002

Kitab Bhavan
Publishers, Distributors, Exporters & Importers
1784, Kalan Mahal, Darya Ganj
New Delhi - 1100 02 (India)

Phone : (91-11) 23277392/93, 23274686, 30906494
website : www.kitabbhavan.com
Email : nasri@vsnl.com
Fax : (91-11) 23263383

ISBN : 81-7151-110-4

First Indian Edition 1988
Second Reprinted 1997
Third Reprinted 2005

Published in India by :
Nusrat Ali Nasri for Kitab Bhavan
1784, Kalan Mahal, Darya Ganj
New Delhi - 1100 02 [India]

Printed in India at :
Nice Printing Press
Khureji Khas, Delhi-110051

PREFACE

IT was in the year 1939 that I went for Pilgrimage for the first time and had an opportunity to meet the late Maulānā 'Ubaidullāh Sindhī in Mecca. He was pleased to see me, took me to his house and showed me some books of Shāh Walīyullāh and encouraged me to study his works. In the same year, after an exile of twenty years, he returned to his homeland where I used to meet him often On every occasion that I met him he impressed upon me the necessity and importance of Shāh Walīyullāh's teachings and their propagation and encouraged me to make a research on him. Those were the days when I was working as a Lecturer in the D. J. Sindh College, Karachi.

As a result of Maulānā's repeated encouragement I began to collect Shāh Ṣāhib's works from wherever I could have them easily, read them and took notes from them, but this course could not continue for long. Had this work, which I have been able to finish this time, been started earlier, it would have never assumed the form and shape in which it is at present before the readers. This is so because a man who does not possess command over the Arabic language and is not fairly aware of its literature cannot understand Shāh Ṣāhib fully. This work was, therefore, discontinued for a number of years.

In the year 1958 when I returned from my third Pilgrimage, the thought of doing research on Shāh

Ṣāḥib suddenly occurred to my mind afresh and firmly settled therein. Consequently, the research work was first published by the Sind University in 1961, in the Sindhi language, and its Urdu version was published by Shāh Walīyullāh Academy in the year 1963. This is its English translation prepared by the author himself. It is more or less a reproduction of the Urdu version with minor changes and some useful additions here and there.

An earnest effort has been made to see that no important item of his teachings is left out of mention, but despite that the book does not claim to have given a detailed account of each and every aspect of the subject discussed in it. However, it can be justly asserted that it has paved the way for further inquiry, and it is hoped that the information supplied in the book will go a long way to quench the thirst of those who are interested in the teachings of Shāh Walīyullāh.

The extraordinary personality of Shāh Walīyullāh is well known to the men of learning. Enough has been written on him in the Urdu language in particular, and the present work also is a step towards that direction. He has clearly mentioned the object he had in view in the "Muqaddimah" of *Ḥujjatullāh-ul-Bālighah*, his *Magnum Opus*. He says there that the modern age demands that the *Sharī'ah* of the Holy Prophet should project itself with convincing arguments. In the same "Muqaddimah" he further states that the best science among all the sciences of the *Sharī'ah* is one which aims at unravelling the secrets underlying the injunctions of religion.

In referring to the same object he says, at some other place, that the existing conditions require a complete change of the old order, and for the fulfilment of that purpose he has been selected.[1]

His teachings unavoidably infuse into the readers the spirit of *Jihād* which, he emphasises, should be retained at all costs and for all times.[2]

This is the third edition in which a few useful additions have been made here and there.

Maulānā 'Ubaidullāh Sindhī has been freely quoted in this book as he was found comparatively far superior to others in giving the correct exposition of Shāh Walīyullāh's teachings and philosophy.

G.N. JALBANI

1. *Fuyūḍ-ul-Ḥaramain*, Mashhad, 44; *Tafhimāt*, Vol. II, p. 120:
- - - عسی ان ینزل علیک الحق فاکا لنظام العالم -

2. *Ḥujjatullāh-ul-Bālighah*, Vol. II, pp. 170-71. The word *Jihād* is of wider significance. Besides actual warfare and adequate preparations for it in advance, it also means fighting against every kind of evil. It has been frequently used in the sense of "revolution" to which a reference has been made in the Chapter on "Socio-Economics". See *Ḥujjatullāh*, Vol. I, pp. 49-50.

CONTENTS

Preface	... ...	v
Muqaddimah	... ...	1
Chapters		
I. The Qur'ān	... ...	6
II. The Tradition	... ...	37
III. The Jurisprudence	... ...	57
IV. The Taṣawwuf	... ...	82
V. The Prophecy	... ...	103
VI. The Sharī'ah	... ...	120
VII. The Politics	... ...	134
VIII. The Socio-Economics	... ...	165
IX. Life After Death	... ...	193
X. Philosophy	... ...	212
XI. Miscellaneous	... ...	230
XII. The Last Word	... ...	239
Bibliography	... ...	242
Index	... ...	248

MUQADDIMAH

QUṬB-UD-DĪN B. 'ABD-UR-RAḤĪM, known as Walīyullāh,[1] was born on the 4th of Shawwāl 1114/1702, in the vicinity of Delhi, in the stormy days of religious decadence when people were divided in sections and sub-sections, each one happy in his own set of beliefs without any regard as to what was true and what was false.[2]

The noblest and the most meritorious task of carrying the Holy War (*Jihād*) against the enemy forces threatening the very foundation of both the religion and the state was forgotten and no more heard of.[3]

Extremely luxurious living of the high and the ruthless persecution of the low and the poor presented a gloomy and sad spectacle, which was in no way better than what it was in the Persian and Roman Empires before Islam.[4]

Herein then was the pressing need of a man to rise and reform both the Church and the State, contaminated to the core as they were, in a manner

1. The name Walīyullāh is given to him because he happened to be the true representation of the Divine Name *al-Waliy*. See *al-Khair al-Kathir*, pp. 70-71. Shāh Walīyullāh, in his writings, calls himself by the name of Aḥmad. He was born in a small village named Pulth, in District Muzaffargarh, U.P. (India).

2. "Muqaddimah," *Ḥujjatullāh-ul-Bālighah*.

3. Ibid., Vol. II, p. 171 :

و كان التقاعد من الجهاد فى مثل هذا الزمان تفويتاً لخير كثير ـ

4. Ibid., Vol. I, p. 105.

consistent with the requirements of the time. Shāh Ṣāḥib, as one learns from his "Autobiography," was an extraordinary genius who finished the course of current sciences within a short period of fifteen years and was graced and entrusted by the Divine Providence with the *Khil'at-i-Fātiḥiyyat*, i.e. the reins to lead and guide for the future.[5]

This two-fold job of the reformation of state and religion could be performed only by one like Shāh Ṣāḥib, who was well grounded in both the exoteric and esoteric sciences.[6]

Analysing the conditions then prevalent, he preferred to fight with his pen rather than with his sword,[7] and launched a vigorous attack, unprejudiced, against all the groups, particularly of the *'Ulamā'*, the so-called learned men deemed as the upholders of Islam, and the Ṣūfīs, the pseudomystics, considered as the repositories of Divine mysteries. The former only whiled away their time and dissipated their energies in hair-splitting over funny interpretations of some of the implications of Law, drawing their deductions in the light of their blind obedience to their *Imāms* whose side they were to support at all cost, the slightest departure from whose teachings in their eyes amounted to a denunciation of the Law-giver himself, thus, giving rise to petty feuds and mutual rivalries and the holding of disputations as a professed fashion of the day; while the latter, being half-educated and

5. *Al-Juz'-ul-Laṭīf.*
6. Ibid.
7. *Al-Tafhīmāt-ul-Ilāhiyyah*, Vol. I, p. 101.

partially influenced by the Hindu Yogism and the Shī'ite tendencies then gaining ground, swam with the current and preferred isolation and detachment. Being much esteemed by the officials and the public, they even began to raise mysticism above the clear practice of the Law (*Sharī'ah*), thus occasioning lethargy, inactivity, and a series of innovations, which had almost sapped the marrow of Islam and cut at its very root.[8]

Such a state of affairs, no doubt, foreshadowed the advent of a reformer, a fulfilment of the Holy Prophet's prayer, in the person of Shāh Walīyullāh to cope with the worsening situation.[9]

Shāh Sāḥib saw the Muslim Empire crippling, the Britishers already casting their covetous eyes on India, from the Bay of Bengal, and the true religion lost among the unworthy and the vicious. He, therefore, armed himself with all the necessary weapons of different sciences in vogue and raised the slogan, "Back to the Qur'ān."

He desired to present Islam in its true form which does not admit extreme rigidity and reserve as shown by the theologians and the misguided mystics (*Ṣūfīs*), and to break away with the old order, replacing it by the new to meet the requirements of the time.[10]

He viewed with clear perspective a new era dawn-

8. Ibid., Vol. I, p. 151 ; *Waṣiyyat-Namāh.*
9. *Al-Tafhīmāt*, Vol. I, p. 40.
10. *Fuyūḍ-ul-Ḥaramain*, Mashhad, 44: وسألونى ما ذا حكم الله فى هذه الساعة ؟ قلت : "فك كل نظام" : *Tafhīmāt*, Vol. II, p. 120 :

ing upon the Muslims and felt that he was selected to deal with a scientific age where people were not disposed to accept everything at its face value, so he aimed at unravelling the secrets and the mysteries of religion to establish the truth of Islam.[11]

Religion, when backed by reason, carries conviction and fortifies wavering faith. Shāh Ṣāḥib, as one can see, was by his nature disposed to proving things on rational basis within the bounds of possibility, but in no way subordinating religion to reason.

He was not a blind imitator. He did not even follow any of the four established schools *in toto*. Rather, he subjected their (*Imāms'*) findings to thorough investigation, both historical and rational. He tests them on the touchstone of the Qur'ān and the *Ḥadīth*; what conforms to them both he accepts, and the rest he rejects outright. The same was the case with his grandson Shāh Ismā'īl, the Martyr.[12]

It indeed goes to his credit that he made a courageous and successful attempt at validating the creeds and dogmas as held and professed by the Ancients, the purity of whose teachings he took pains to preserve, and set at naught the objections of the *Ma'qūliyyīn* (rationalists) with reasonable arguments and positive proofs.[13]

His works are many but his *Ḥujjatullāh-ul-Bālighah*

11. *Al-Juz'-ul-Laṭīf*; *ad-Durr-uth-Thamīn fī Mubashsharāt-in-Nabiyyil-Amīn*.

12. Sayyid 'Abd-ul-Ḥayy al-Ḥasanī, *ath-Thaqāfat-ul-Islāmiyyah fi'l-Hind*.

13. *Al-Juz'-ul-Laṭīf*.

is unique among them all. It is indeed an encyclopaedia of religious sciences. He died on the 29th of Muḥarram 1176/1763, when he was sixty-one years and four months old.[14]

14. *Malfūẓāt Shāh 'Abd-ul-'Azīz.*

Chapter I

THE QUR'ĀN

IN the days of Shāh Walīyullāh, the official language was Persian, which was much popular and commonly understood. As such, the need was felt to render the Word of God into that language for the benefit of the masses. The conditions at that time were in no way favourable, but Shāh Ṣāḥib, regardless of all the consequences, translated the Qur'ān into simple Persian, with a few brief comments here and there.[1]

The Muslims in general were under the wrong impression that the sheer conventional reading of the Qur'ān fulfils its due right, and this was indeed the main reason that led Shāh Ṣāḥib to undertake its translation. What distinguishes this translation is that in quantity, generality and particularity it is identical with the original text, though at some places, for reader's facility, this procedure has been left off.[2]

In India at least Shāh Ṣāḥib's *Fatḥ-ur-Raḥmān* is the first version in Persian, and his occasional comments on it are significant and useful and are an index to the state of mind and thought, with which

1. *Muqaddimah dar Fann-i-Tarjimah-i-Qur'ān* ; Maulānā Muḥammad Raḥim Bakhsh, *Ḥayāt-i-Wali*, pp. 418-19.
2. *Muqaddimah dar Fann-i-Tarjimah-i-Qur'ān*.

he understood the Qur'ān.[3]

Independent Study. Shāh Walīyullāh was of the view that the Qur'ān should be studied independently without reference to a commentary, and it is the duty of the teacher to solve the difficulty of his student wherever necessary, as this procedure would brighten up his brain and give him encouragement towards independent study.

As the first step towards this, he suggests that the child in the beginning should be taught such few elementary books on grammar as he may be able to digest properly, and afterwards he may be made to read some books on history or ethics in Arabic. In addition to these he should also be apprised of some of the difficult structural forms of the language. Thus, when the student gains command over the language he may be allowed to translate the Qur'ān himself without consulting a commentary. However, care should be taken to see that wherever the meaning of the Qur'ān does not become clear to him without first knowing the occasion of revelation, or without understanding the text's grammatical construction, it should be discussed with him in detail. And later when he is free from his day's lesson, he may be instructed to supplement it by reading an equal portion from *Tafsīr Jalālain*.[4]

3. Sayyid 'Abd-ul-Ḥayy al-Ḥasanī, *ath-Thaqāfat-ul-Islāmiyyah fi'l-Hind*; Maulānā 'Ubaidullāh Sindhī, *Ilhām-ur-Raḥmān*, p. 72.

Makhdūm Nūḥ (d. 998/1589) of Hala, Sind, was the first person in the Indo-Pakistan subcontinent who translated the Qur'ān into Persian, and this translation has been published.

4. *Wasiyyat-Nāmah*.

This method of teaching the Qur'ānic text without the help of a commentary was first introduced by Shāh 'Abd-ur-Raḥīm and then faithfully continued by his worthy son, Shāh Walīyullāh, but was unfortunately ignored and given up later on.[5]

It has been observed that in studying the commentators' works, reader's attention is not infrequently diverted from the Word of God towards the explanations advanced by the people of his stock. And if he is to devote himself to the reading of commentaries, it will take away almost his whole time and give him no opportunity whatsoever to concentrate upon the Qur'ān. Experience has shown that plain and independent thinking over it often results in the emergence of new ideas and meanings. This probably was the main reason why Shāh Walīyullāh used to teach first the Qur'ān lesson before commencing the *Ṣiḥāḥ-Sittah* known as *Daur-i-Ḥadīth* in those days.[6]

It is indeed a matter of regret that the thorough knowledge of grammar, logic, scholasticism and rhetoric is considered now-a-days a prerequisite towards the understanding of the Qur'ān Consequently the acquisition of all these sciences allows no saving of time for the student to think over and meditate upon the Word of God. In fact, the real teaching of the Qur'ān is never being imparted in our religious institutions at present and the teaching of its commentaries has been substituted for it.[7]

5. *Anfās-ul-'Ārifīn*, p. 86. 6. *Malfūẓāt Shāh 'Abd-ul-'Azīz.*

7. Maulānā 'Ubaidullāh Sindhī, *Qur'ān Pāk kā Muṭāla'ah kaisay kiyā jā'ay*, p. 33.

That is why Shāh Ṣāḥib says at one place that the preliminaries for the understanding of the Qur'ān should be read as preliminaries and not treated as an independent science to be studied in detail.[8]

The teaching of the Qur'ān's commentaries should always be considered to be quite different from the teaching of the Qur'ān itself. Different commentaries have been written at different times according to their requirements, while the Holy Prophet is reported to have said that the expansion of the knowledge of the Qur'ān will continue up to the Day of Judgment; but in spite of that we have contented ourselves with the past commentaries and have given up further research and inquiry.

For a correct approach towards the study of the Qur'ān, Shāh Ṣāḥib composed a treatise *al-Fauz-ul-Kabīr fī Uṣūl it-Tafsīr* and this Persian composition of his is undoubtedly unique in itself, as the like of it has never been produced by anyone before him. In this work he has laid down the principles to be followed in the study of the Qur'ān.[9]

Subject-matter. While explaining the principles of *Tafsīr* he has divided the subject-matter of the Holy Qur'ān into five categories.

(1) The Science of Injunctions, which pertains to what is Incumbent, Approved, Disapproved and Forbidden, whether they be in connection with worship or dealings of man with man, household admin-

8. *Tafhīmāt*, Vol. I, pp. 214-15.

9. Sayyid 'Abd-ul-Ḥayy al-Ḥasanī, *Nuzhat-ul-Khawāṭir wa Bahjat-ul-Masāmi' wa'n-Nawāẓir*, Vol. VI, p. 401

istration and state politics.

(2) The Science of Disputations, which relates to the four misguided groups, namely, Jews, Christians, Polytheists and the Hypocrites.

(3) The Science pertaining to the Divine Wonders, wherein the attention of the people is drawn to the wondrous signs of the Almighty in Nature.

(4) The Science pertaining to the important occasions; in that an account of those occasions is given on which the obedient were helped and blessed and the disobedient were taken to task and punished.

(5) The Science concerning Death, wherein is the mention of the horrors of death and of the effect on man of the events which are to follow it.

He clearly asserts that the topics treated in the Qur'ān are confined to these five categories only.

This kind of division of the contents of the Qur'ān is indeed the result of Shāh Ṣāḥib's own investigation.

Method of Explanation. The explanation of these five sciences is given according to the style with which the ancient Arabs were familiar, and not according to the technique adopted by the later academicians who in their writings observe subject-wise arrangement, summarisation and systematic treatment.[10]

The Divine method is contrary to this order.

10. *Al-Fauz-ul-Kabīr fi Uṣūl-it-Tafsir*, p. 3 :

و بیان این علوم بروش تقریر عرب اول واقع شد نہ بروش تقریر متاخران - - - -

Ḥujjatullāh-ul-Bālighah, Vol. I, pp. 55-56; *Kalimāt-i-Ṭayyibāt*, p. 166; *Qurrat-ul-'Ainain fi Tafḍil-ish-Shaikhain*, p. 312.

Whatever God found useful and beneficial for His people at a particular moment, He revealed, regardless of what preceded or followed it. It is here that the style of the Qur'ān differs from that of the Pentateuch and the Gospel.

For example, the Arabs used to demonstrate their eloquence in the form of their odes which they always began with the amatory preludes, in which they mentioned some touching scenes and important events. This in reality was their old practice. The very same practice has been followed in some of the verses of the Holy Qur'ān itself.[11]

In the Introduction it has been mentioned that Shah Ṣāḥib never accepted anything unless it was found in conformity with the Book of God and the Tradition of the Prophet. Accordingly at times, he is not found to be in agreement with some of the views of the commentators in general. His way of approach to the Qur'ān is rather peculiar and that is what accounts for his apparent difference in views.

Arrangement. The majority of commentators, for example, have linked up almost every verse of the Qur'ān with one happening or the other and have taken that particular happening to be the cause of its revelation; while in fact, the real purpose behind the revelation was the purification of the hearts of men, the rejection of their wrong notions and the eradication of all their acts of evil.[12]

This may not give rise to any misunderstanding

11. *Al-Fauz-ul-Kabir*, pp. 28-29. 12. Ibid., p. 3.

that the Divine Book is in any way wanting in literary beauties and systematic arrangement. The contention of Shāh Walīyullāh is that the present-day logical treatment of the subjects under which all the items pertaining to a certain subject-matter are treated under an exclusive heading, and not repeated elsewhere, is certainly not found in the Qur'ān. In other words, each one of these five sciences mentioned before is treated repeatedly throughout the Book.[13]

As an illustration, if one were to look to the verse "Or do they say, He has forged it? Say: If I had forged it, I bear my own sin, and I am free of the sins of which you are guilty," he will find it having no connection whatsoever with what precedes it or follows it, as this verse apparently looks somewhat out of place in the context of the story of the Prophet Noah. But if one ponders over it one will come to the conclusion that this verse here is quite appropriate and most befitting the occasion. The condition of the Meccan polytheists at that time was just the same as that of Noah's people, as they did not obey their Prophet and suffered punishment and perished; similarly, here in this verse a warning is being given to the enemies of the Holy Prophet to learn a lesson from it, mend their ways and give up opposition.[14]

Again, if this verse, "Verily, by thy life (O Prophet), in their intoxication, they wander in distraction to and fro," be taken into consideration, it will be found to have no link with its pros and cons,

13. Ibid., pp. 6, 32-33.
14. *Fatḥ-ur-Raḥmān*, Sūrah Hūd, verse 35.

being outwardly a mere interruption in the narration of the Prophet Lot; but here also as before the verse has been brought in to serve as a warning to the idolaters of Mecca whose life in no way differed from that of Lot's people, so that they may desist from disobeying the Prophet, otherwise they would go down the way their ancestors had gone. By the insertion of this verse in the middle as in the preceding case, it is the link in meaning which is aimed at rather than the link of narration.[15]

To maintain this link in meaning intact, a departure has also been made on some occasions from the regularity of the style itself, as is illustrated by the verse, "Thy Lord doth know that thou standest forth (to prayer) nigh two-thirds of the night," right up to its end. Now, the style of this verse is different from the rest of the verses, but here also it has been incorporated as the purpose and meaning of it have close relationship with the whole of the chapter.[16]

A similar example is afforded in the verse, "And We have set none but angels as guardians of the Fire." Herein also the mutual relationship of the verses in meaning is given consideration to, and the style which otherwise continued throughout the chapter has been discontinued here, as the occasion required, to dispel the doubts that the unbelievers had regarding the nineteen angels of Hell.[17]

No doubt the commentators, says Maulānā

15. Ibid., Sūrah Ḥajar, verse 72.
16. Ibid., Sūrah Muzzammil, verse 20.
17. Ibid., Sūrah Muddaththir, verse 31; *al-Fauz-ul-Kābir*, p. 28.

'Ubaidullāh, have been able to establish a link between the first twenty-five verses of the Chapter "Baqarah". Their argument is that God has first made a mention of the believers, then of the unbelievers and followed it with the mention of the hypocrites; and because a thing is always known better by its opposite, so all the twenty-five verses are in a way in praise of the believers. But it is a fact that these very commentators have failed in suggesting the link of the verse that follows them: "God disdains not to use the similitude of things lowest as well," with what preceded or followed it.[18]

Again, in Sūrah "Qiyāmah" the verses from 16 to 19, "Move not thy Tongue, concerning the (Qur'ān) to make haste therewith," seem to have no correspondence with the preceding and the succeeding verses, but here also the digression has been made because of the requirement of the occasion. When this Sūrah was being revealed to the Prophet, he, seeing its extraordinary eloquence, attempted to commit it to memory, whereupon he was advised to remain patient and give up memorisation.

However, Shāh Walīyullāh is of the view that the rigid system of arrangement and coherence which is being followed in the composition works now-a-days is not followed in the Qur'ān.

Abrogation. The question of the Abrogation and the Abrogated Verses is rather confusing, the confusion being caused by the divergent views which the Ancients and the Moderns have about its terminology.

18. *Ilhām-ur-Rahmān*, p. 84.

What can be gathered after proper sifting from the speech of the Companions and their immediate followers is that they took the word "abrogation" (*naskh*) in its literal sense, namely, suppression of one thing by the other, and not in the technical sense taken by the Jurists.[19]

Even in the case of technical abrogation, the rule is that information should be first gathered about the occasion on which the verses were revealed, but the commentators and theologians at times only take the unanimous opinion of the Ancients and the general consensus of the religious leaders (*Imāms*) to be the sign of abrogation and then stoutly maintain that view. It is, however, possible that the verifier of the verse be different from the verifier of the consensus of the opinion.[20]

But as the learned doctors of Islam were not found in agreement among themselves as to the exact number of abrogated verses, this question caused enough confusion to the mind and the thought of the Muslims. For example, a reader of the Qur'ān takes a certain meaning from a certain verse, but the thought that this same verse might have been abrogated by some other verse sometimes occurs in his mind, with the result that he finds an excuse for not acting upon that verse.

When any injunction which was first stated in general form, and afterwards on some other occasion

19. *Al-Fauz-ul-Kabir*, p. 15 ; *al-Khair-ul-Kathir*, p. 126.
20. *Al-Fauz-ul-Kabir*, pp. 37-38.

was particularised, or when something in the beginning was expressed summarily, and later on in details, then, from the language point of view, it used to be said that the latter has abrogated the former. This actually was the meaning which the Ancients gave to the word "abrogation". The abrogation of this kind does exist in the Holy Qur'ān; for example, the Meccan Chapters generally mention the universals and the principles and the Chapters revealed at Medina discuss them with details and give comments.[21]

On account of this difference among the commentators about the significance of the term "*naskh*" (abrogation), the number of abrogated verses rose considerably. Imām Suyūṭī, however, after effecting a suitable reduction brought them to nineteen only. But Shāh Walīyullāh has given the solution of fourteen of them and considers only five as abrogated.[22]

A thoughtful consideration leads us to conclude that he did not believe in abrogation in the Qur'ān, because the solution of those five verses (comparatively simple) is not difficult to seek. This can be done in the way that the abrogating verse be taken as "more deserving" and the abrogated as "less deserving" or that we may take one as pointing to an "obligatory statute" (*'Aẓīmah*) and the other to "permission" (*Rukhṣah*).[23]

21. Maulānā 'Ubaidullāh Sindhī, *Shāh Waliyullāh aur Un kā Falsafah*, pp. 72-73.

22. *Al-Fauz-ul-Kabir*, p. 18.

23. Maulānā 'Ubaidullāh Sindhī, *Shāh Waliyullāh aur Un kā Falsafah*, pp. 72-78.

According to the above explanation the meaning of abrogation does not remain the same as taken by the Jurists, i.e. precluding the verse from all practical purposes. Shāh Walīyullāh, however, considers that the question of abrogation is subject to individual reasoning and in this he does not agree with their views.[24]

The Qur'ānic verse, "For those who can do it is a ransom, the feeding of one that is indigent,"[25] has been considered by many as abrogated, as outwardly it means that those who are able to keep the fast but do not do so can be absolved of fasting if they pay the ransom, while on the other hand none shares that belief, and according to them this verse had been abrogated by the verse, "So every one of you who is present (at his home) during that month should spend it in fasting."[26]

In fact, this verse is not an abrogated one, as it means that people who are able to feed must feed one poor man. Here the pronoun has been used before its antecedent because, in respect of rank, the antecedent is placed before and the inchoative has been brought after it, as it is a common noun. The famous grammarian al-Farrā' is also of the opinion that the pronoun here does not refer to the fast (*Ṣiyām*). Further, it has been used here in the masculine gender because by *fidyah* (ransom) is meant the fast, and by food the alms of breaking the fast (*ṣadaqat-ul-fiṭr*).

Now the actual arrangement of the verse stands

24. *Tafhimāt*, Vol. II, p. 173.
25. Sūrah al-Baqarah, verse 184.
26. Ibid., verse 185.

as follows : "A ransom, the feeding of a poor, is the duty of those who are able to do so" (*Fidyatun ṭa'ām miskīnin 'alal-ladhīn yuṭiqūnahū*). Accordingly, the correct meaning of the verse is that he who is able to feed, it is obligatory on him to do so, in order that his fast become complete and he himself become free from the vice of niggardliness.[27]

The field of sciences that the Qur'ān covers is very vast and extensive and Shāh Walīyullāh fortunately possessed a copious share of these sciences and was well acquainted with their fundaments and consequences. Here he occupies the same position as enjoyed by an independent interpreter in the school of thought he belongs to (*al-Mujtahid fi'l-Madhhab*).[28]

So well grounded was he in the exegesis of the Divine Scripture that he claims to infer from it directly all that has come in the Tradition regarding the canonical prayers. God, for example, speaking of the prayers says in the general form, "Glorify the name of thy Lord, most high"; and as, "Sing the glory of thy Lord." From these, Shāh Ṣāḥib points out, the Prophet concluded the appointed times.

At another place we have, "Stand up," "Extol," "Recite what is being revealed to thee," "Bend," and "Prostrate"; from these, he says, the Prophet deduced that they form the pillars of the prayer.

Similarly, where God takes oaths of certain things

27. *Al-Fauz-ul-Kabīr*, p. 16; *al-Khair-ul-Kathīr*, pp. 105-06; *al-Muṣaffā*, Vol. I, pp. 230-32.

28. *Al-Fauz-ul-Kabīr*, p. 35; Sayyid 'Abd-ul-Ḥayy al-Ḥasanī, *Nuzhat-ul-Khawāṭir*, Vol. VI, p. 401.

we have the words, "By the break of the day," "By the nights twice five," "By the ruddy glow of sunset."[29] In his opinion, the Prophet drew the conclusion here that these verses refer to the times of the prayer. But the way followed by the Prophet in inference is radically different from the one followed by the Jurists.[30]

Shāh Walīyullāh is certainly not agreeable to the views held by those commentators who assert that the "allegorical verses" are beyond the scope of man's understanding. He, on the contrary, opines that those "who are firmly rooted in knowledge" can comprehend them all right and similarly the intelligent students after protracted efforts and serious thinking can come up to the level of the "firmly-rooted"

If, on the other hand, the comprehension of the allegorical verses be taken as beyond the pale of human imagination, then the understanding of the Qur'ān will remain incomplete. And this is likely to give rise to many a misunderstanding in the minds of its readers, which would then be the cause of their diversion from the practical purposes enshrined in the Message of God.[31]

In the verse, "None knows its interpretation but God and those who are firmly-rooted in knowledge,"[32] the majority of commentators have allowed necessary

29. Sūrah al-Fajr, verses 1-2; Sūrah al-Inshiqāq, verse 18.

30. *Al-Khair-ul-Kathir*, p. 87.

31. Maulānā 'Ubaidullāh Sindhī, *Shāh Waliyullāh aur Un kā Falsafah*, pp. 58-59.

32. Sūrah Āl-i-'Imrān, verse 6.

pause (*waqf-i-lāzim*) after "but God," while there are others like Shāh Walīyullāh, Mujāhid and Imām Shāfi'ī who do not make a break at the point here, but run the two sentences together.

When the Holy Prophet was asked by the Jews about the spirit, the reply given to them was, "The knowledge which has been given to you is but little." This very verse definitely throws light upon the fact that the knowledge of the reality of the spirit is not beyond the reach of human intellect, even though it may be known to very few.[33]

The science of the Abbreviated Letters is also a branch of philosophy and Shāh Walīyullāh has taken an active part in it. When "nūn" and "fā" occur in a triliteral word, it gives the meaning of "*khurūj*" (outgoing, disbursement, expenditure, etc.) as the words "*nafar*," "*nafath*," "*nafad*" and "*nafadh*" indicate. Sometimes the Arabs, by a replacement of an approximate letter in the word, use it in different meanings, like "*dakk*" (breaking, crushing) and "*daqq*" (to become thin and refined), "*lajj*" (persistence, continuation in litigation) and "*lazz*" (cleaving, adherence, etc.).

The meaning of "Alif-Lām-Mīm," for example, is that the unspecified unseen has become specified in relation to this unclean world. By "Hamzah" here is meant the unseen of the immaterial world. "Lām" refers to specification, and "Mīm" points to the unclean matter in which different realities have united

33. *Ḥujjatullāh-ul-Bālighah*, Vol. I, p. 18 ; *Hama'āt, Hama'* 20, p. 62. Qur'ān, Sūrah Banī Isrā'īl, verse 85.

together, and become determined. This whole abbreviation alludes to the sheer flow of beneficence towards this world of restriction and limitation.

He agrees with the commentators that the abbreviated letters indicate the names of the Chapters (*Suwar*) they occur in, but at the same time maintains the view that they refer to some universal attribute rather than the particular one, just as Imām Bukhārī has named his book as *Jāmi' aṣ-Ṣaḥīḥ al-Musnad fī Ḥadīth Rasūlillāh.*[34] However, he admits that the knowledge of the abbreviation is not within the scope of regular speech or general discourse.[35]

Occasion of Revelation. As regards the "occasion of revelation" in the Holy Qur'ān, Shāh Ṣāḥib's contention is that the "occasion of revelation" is of two kinds. In one, the verse revealed clearly points out to a certain happening, while in the other, in spite of having an implied reference to some occasion, it is general in its application, and it is the general meaning that is counted there without being restricted to the particular happening that gave rise to its revelation.[36]

Although the theologians "in the principles of Jurisprudence" have unanimously made it clear that if a verse is revealed in the general form and the commentators cited a certain happening in connection with its revelation, then it is the general meaning that is to be taken into account, but, in spite of that unani-

34. *Al-Fauz-ul-Kabir*, p. 41 ; *Hawāmi'*.
35. *Al-Fauz-ul-Kabir*, p. 41 ; *al-Khair-ul-Kathir*, p. 130.
36. *Al-Fauz-ul-Kabir*, p. 35.

mity, this procedure was not scrupulously followed.

If one were to turn to any commentary (*Tafsīr*) of the Qur'ān one will find that every verse has been associated with one occasion or the other. As an example, the commentators usually say that this verse refers to Abū Jahl and that one to the merits of Abū Bakr and so on, with the result that both the teacher and the taught are generally found occupied with the reading of those particular cases. To confine the whole of the Qur'ān to particular occasions instead of universal purposes and ideas has resulted in its not proving effective as a whole in the life of man.[37]

The ancient commentators, under the idea that Traditions having connection with the various verses of the Qur'ān be collected or that some example be given about the general injunctions, have mentioned their occasion of revelation, while as a matter of fact there was no such need of it. The particular occasion which became the focus of their attention and study had nothing to do with the occasion of revelation.[38]

There was, of course, a small number of verses which explicitly referred to some happenings before or during the life of the Holy Prophet, and because of that reference they call for fuller account. It is, therefore, necessary for us to give the explanation of the Qur'ānic sciences in such a manner that there should be no need to take the trouble of mentioning the particular happenings.[39]

37. Maulānā 'Ubaidullāh Sindhī, *Shāh Walīyullāh aur Un kā Falsafah*, pp. 37-38.

38. *Al-Fauz-ul-Kabīr*, p. 3.

39. Ibid., pp. 3, 12, 20.

In the Chapter (*Sūrah*) Muddaththir, for example, from verse 11 to verse 25 there is given the psychological analysis of a capitalist To associate these verses with one unbeliever Walīd b. Mughīrah only is not enough; these verses have general application, and every person in every age must take stock of his own self and see how far he is affected by that capitalistic mentality.[40]

It has been proved and verified that whenever the Commpanions and their immediate followers say that a particular verse has been revealed in connection with such and such happening, their intention, generally speaking, is to point out the picture of its verifier or to mention a particular happening which that verse on account of its universality comprises, no matter whether the happening which they take to be the cause of revelation occurred before or after its revelation.

From the assessment of facts and proper scrutiny thereof, it is concluded that the occasion of revelation can be subjected to independent reasoning.[41]

Even in the narration of a happening, the rule is that it should be narrated as it was heard without the projection of one's personal view. But some of the ancient commentators having adopted their personal view as a guide and, taking for it one or the other suitable occasion for granted, have given the explanation based on mere probability. This naturally created a doubt in the minds of the later commenta-

40. Maulānā 'Ubaidullāh Sindhī, *Qurānī Dastūr-i-Inqilāb.*
41. *Al-Fauz-ul-Kabir*, p. 35 :
ازین تحقیق دانسته شد که اجتهاد را درین قسم دخلی هست ۔

tors, because in those olden days the mode of explanation was not so systematic and plain as it is today. Thus, the explanation given only by way of a probability was generally taken as one based on conclusiveness.[42]

A thorough investigation shows that many discussions even among the Companions were held for the sake of scientific research and ascertainment. For example, the remarks of Ibn 'Abbās about the verse, "Wipe your head and your feet up to ankles," "I do not find in the Book of God save the wiping, but they (the people) have refused else but washing," were only for the sake of ascertainment and scientific inquiry into religious matters. Here he has never been of the view that wiping is an incumbent duty. On the contrary, he held the doctrine of washing the feet in ablution. But people who were not well aware of the day-to-day affairs of the Ancients, taking it (wiping) to be the view of Ibn 'Abbās, had declared it as his profession.[43]

This (significance of the occasion of revelation), however, is not a new idea of Shāh Walīyullāh, but what goes to his credit is that he gave added encouragement to it, renewed his support, gave publicity to it and disseminated it among his pupils and followers.

In explaining grammatical points of the Qur'ān, some have followed the line of Sībawaih, while others have accepted Farrā' as an authority, with the result that wherever they find a grammatical point against

42. *Al-Fauz-ul-Kabir*, pp. 35-36. 43. Ibid., p. 36

their own professed beliefs they begin to give one or the other interpretation, however far-fetched and remote it may be. Here Shāh Ṣāḥib's advice is that it behoves the learned to follow that point which may tally with the context and be found more sound. Neither Sībawaih nor Farrā' should be taken as a deciding instrument there.[44]

Meccan and Medina Chapters. The enemies of Islam always object that in the Meccan chapters an individual being is addressed to reform and improve himself, but in the chapters revealed at Medina the public in general is addressed. In other words, the apparent difference which they find in the life of the Prophet spent both at Mecca and Medina has become a cause of their objection. Their saying is that as long as the Prophet was there in Mecca, he used to live a life of a preacher and an instructor, but as soon as he set foot in Medina, he turned out to be a law-giver and a ruler of a state.

The answer to their objection is that during his stay at Mecca, the prevailing conditions were not such as to call for an open *Jihād* (Holy War) and the use of force, although the secret *Jihād* was started even in Mecca as is corroborated by the verse; "See they not that We gradually reduce the land (in their control) from its outlying borders?" It is, therefore, that Shāh Walīyullāh, against the majority of the commentators and historians, is of the opinion that this verse is a Meccan revelation. It is evident from this verse that during the Prophet's ministry at Mecca,

44. Ibid., p. 39.

the domination of Islam continued spreading throughout Arabia and the territory held by the enemies went on diminishing day by day, because the various tribes such as Aslam, Ghifār, Juhainah, Muzainah, and certain tribes of Yemen had entered into the fold of Islam.[45]

Thus, the objection of the enemies that the intention of waging war and extending his political power beyond the borders of the Arabian Peninsula occurred to the Prophet only after he came to Medina is utterly groundless. His life at Medina was the consummation of his Meccan life. At Mecca his movement was based on party system which later on in Medina first became national and then international. The historians in general link the beginning of the building of the Islamic State with the Prophet's arrival at Medina, a theory which is untenable and hardly correct as is shown by the Qur ānic verse mentioned before.[46]

Congruity. Here it is necessary to remove certain misunderstandings. We find that there is a mention, in the Meccan chapters, of the Jews believing the Holy Qur'ān and in the chapters revealed at Medina of their disbelieving it. It is so because as long as the Prophet was there at Mecca he had never invited the Jews to embrace the new faith. It is, therefore, that they believed it to be true and accepted its law as binding upon the Arabs. But later, when the Prophet migrated to Medina, he called upon them to accept Islam which they did not like and turned out to be

45. *Fatḥ-ur-Raḥmān*, Sūrah Ra'd, verse 41.

46. Maulānā 'Ubaidullāh Sindhī, *Shāh Walīyullāh aur Un kā Falsafah*, pp. 54-55.

his enemies to oppose him.[47]

Likewise the opponents of Islam oftentimes, out of sheer prejudice, criticise the Book of God. They have questioned the appropriateness of the meaning of the verse, "For the iniquity of the Jews, We made unlawful for them certain things, good and pleasing which had been lawful for them."[48]

Their objection is that there is contradiction in this verse, as it is not compatible with the true fact, because the flesh of camel and of the animals having claws was already forbidden for them according to the Pentateuch. To say that when they rejected the Prophet Jesus the good and pleasing things were made unlawful for them as a consequence thereof, is in no way consistent with the true fact. For their disobedience of the Prophet Jesus they should have been penalised in some other way.

Shāh Ṣāḥib's reply to this objection is that by forbidding them the good things is meant their deprivation of that condition of prosperity which they were favoured with before: in other words, kingdom, prophethood, victory, etc., which accompanied them for long. This verse is like the other two verses which when read together would be found to have one and the same context: "And they were covered with humiliation and misery,"[49] and "There is a ban on any population which We have destroyed."[50]

47. *Fatḥ-ur-Raḥmān*, Sūrah al-An'ām, verse 114.
48. Ibid., Sūrah an-Nisā', verse 160.
49. Ibid., Sūrah al-Baqarah, verse 61.
50. Ibid., Sūrah al-Anbiyā', verse 95.

This is what actually happened. The Jews were promised the land of Canaan and that promise was fulfilled with them. They came and settled there permanently, but, in spite of that, they did not give up their obstinacy and began flouting the commandments of God, with the result that their disobedience became the cause of national disaster. They were driven away from their dwellings and then dispersed, wandering from place to place, despised and hated. They were carried in captivity to Assyria, then came under Persian yoke and afterwards under the yoke of Greeks, Romans and Arabs.

Changes. There are oft-repeated references in the Holy Qur'ān to the "changes" the people of the Book were making in the Divine Scriptures. From them it is generally interpreted that those changes had been made in the text of the Books themselves, but, when looked into with an eye of impartiality, this kind of interpretation is found invalid and unsound.

In explaining the significance of "change" (*Taḥrīf*) in the Divine Scriptures, Shāh Walīyullāh says that the people of the Book used to make wrong interpretations of the text, turning away from its obvious meaning in order to suit their own purpose and then passing them on as textual and real. At times, they indulged in making vicious inferences and perverse deductions and then declared them as the original injunctions of the Gospel and the Pentateuch.[51]

The Holy Prophet in reference to that kind of

51. *Al-Khair-ul-Kathīr*, p. 128 ; *Fatḥ-ur-Raḥmān*, Sūrah Āl-i-'Imrān, verse 78 ; *al-Fauz-ul-Kabīr*, p. 9.

malpractice has already warned that very soon persons will appear who would assign different names to wine-drinking and fornication and then show them as lawful in the Book of God. This kind of change is rampant everywhere.[52]

Sometimes the speech (*kalām*) was found capable of two meanings. The translator took one meaning, while the speaker had the other in mind. This was also one of the main causes of the changes that took place in the Sacred Books.[53]

However, Imām Bukhārī, Shaikh-ul-Islām Ibn Taimīyyah and Shāh Walīyullāh do not believe that changes took place in the very text of the Pentateuch.[54]

In the Pentateuch, for example, the punishment prescribed for the fornicator was stoning, but the Jews, on account of their own personal interests which they had to safeguard changed that punishment into blackening his face and giving him a few lashes. Once a case of fornication occurred among them. They sent that fornicator to the Prophet just to ascertain the nature of punishment he would suggest. The Prophet awarded him stoning. The man was then stoned by them, and to this incidence refers the verse: "They change the words from their (right) times and places."[55]

In spite of all this, it would be absolutely wrong

52. *Al-Budūr-ul-Bāzighah*, p. 127; *Tafhimāt*, Vol. II, pp. 134-35.
53. *Al-Muqaddimah fi Qawānin-it-Tarjimah.*
54. *Al-Fauz-ul-Kabir*, p. 7; Maulānā 'Ubaidullāh Sindhī, *Shāh Waliyullāh aur Un kā Falsafah*, p. 104.
55. *Fatḥ-ur-Raḥmān*, Sūrah al-Mā'idah, verse 44.

to believe that the Pentateuch and the Gospel have gone under such a change that no injunction of theirs is worth acceptance. Had it been so, the Qur'ān would not have so frequently invited them to follow their own Books, and would not have accused them of their straying away from them. Our *'Ulamā'* generally want to see those Books as well preserved and secure as is the Qur'ān, and it seems to have settled in their minds that the former Divine Books were revealed after the manner of the Qur'ān. This conception of theirs is wrong. The fact is that all the Heavenly Books revealed before the Qur'ān were revealed after the type of the Divine Tradition (*Ḥadīth Qudsī*), which contained not only the results of the spiritual experiences of those prophets, but an account of their sayings and doings as well.

The learned among the followers of that religion were collecting the Divine Book on the strength of their individual reasoning, and the individual reasoning does not always lead to the right conclusion. Naturally, the Divine Message that passed through them consisted of not only the words and meanings which the Prophet received directly, but also had a blend of their disciples' individual reasoning. In this respect (where the Prophet received them directly) the ten commandments of the Pentateuch and the Sermons of Jesus in the Gospel can be cited as an example.[56]

Revelation, the words and meanings of which

56. Maulānā 'Ubaidullāh Sindhī, *Shāh Walīyullāh aur Un kā Falsafah*, pp. 99-104.

should have remained safe and secure in the form and shape it came does not exist with the exception of a very few portions, anywhere in any religion. A book which could not survive the passage of time and could not continue well preserved and jealously guarded by its followers cannot be called a Heavenly Book; such a one is only a Scroll wherein the followers of that religion collected the knowledge and guidance of their Prophet. The status of that Scroll is similar to the status of the Traditions of Bukhārī and Muslim with us.[57]

According to Shāh Walīyullāh, Ibn 'Abbās's commentary on the Qur'ān, which is the earliest, is more authentic and reliable. In the explanation of the rarities (*gharā'ib*) of the Qur'ān, this commentary is considered to be the best. It enshrines both the solutions of language difficulties and the occasion of revelation. But, in spite of all these merits, Shāh Ṣāḥib is not prepared to accept its explanation everywhere *in toto*.[58]

An example of the difference in approach is illustrated by the verse, "Move not thy tongue concerning the (Qur'ān) to make haste therewith; it is for Us to collect it and to read it, but when We have read it, follow thou its reading; nay more, it is for Us to explain it (and make it clear)."[59]

57. *Saṭa'āt, Sāṭa'* 21, p. 16 :
کتب الاهی پیش از قرآن همه به روش حدیث قدسی بوده اند -

58 *As-Sirr-ul-Maktūm fi Asbāb Tadwin-il-'Ulūm.*

59. *Al-Fauz-ul-Kabir*, p. 37 ; Qur'ān, Sūrah al-Qiyāmah, verses 16-19 ; *Fatḥ-ul-Khabir*, p. 2.

The explanation of this verse as given by Ibn 'Abbās is as follows: "The Prophet had to exert hard during the time of revelation. He used to hear it and read it without raising his voice; that is why he was asked to stop moving his tongue By 'collection' is meant the retention of it in the heart, and by 'reading' is meant his (Prophet's) reading. 'On Us is the explanation of it' has again reference to the explanation of it to the Prophet."[60]

Here Shāh Walīyullāh remarks that, when the original Tradition in connection with this verse is taken into account, it will be found that the meaning of the word *Jam'* is an outcome of Ibn 'Abbās's personal view. He has fixed the tenor of the words "collection," "reading" and "explanation" as one and the same. And to derive such meaning from the verse, "Then it is for Us to explain it," which should not have taken place without reasonable delay is again far from rhetorics, because the word *thumma* in Arabic is used for some delay. To take the approximate meaning of all the three words is away from rhetorics.

Accordingly, the proper explanation would be to take "On Us is its collection" to mean that "the collection of the Qur'ān into books is Our responsibility," and to take "its reading" to mean that the followers of the Prophet would be 'strengthened by Us to keep to its constant reading and to commit it to their memory." In other words, God says to His

60 *Izālat-ul-Khafā'*, Vol. I, p. 50.

Prophet to give up exertion and not to worry about the retention of it in the heart. Its collection into books and then supporting its followers towards its reading is a matter exclusively of Our concern. Then "On Us is its explanation" be taken to mean that it is Our duty to elucidate the Qur'ān, and in this direction, We in every age would be preparing and helping a group of persons to understand its language and the occasion of revelation, etc., and this thing will take place after your death.

Where some of the verses resemble one another, it is necessary, while commenting, to take the fullest advantage of the Tradition of the Prophet, as he is the real exponent of the Qur'ān. What is learnt from the Tradition is that the promise which God held out for the preservation of the Qur'ān will be fulfilled in the form of its collection into books and in the engagement of its followers in its recitation and comprehension. The Tradition, "The water will not wash it off," refers to that.[61]

Another point to be borne in mind is that the words "*Jam'ahū wa qur'ānahū*" (the collection and the reading of it) have been brought together at one place by the conjunctive "*wa*" (and), while the word "*bayānahū*" (its explanation) is preceded by "*thumma*" (then) which comes for delay. This suggests that the reading of the Qur'ān will go hand in hand with its collection while its explanation will take place afterwards. This is what actually happened.

61. Ibid., Vol. I, pp. 50-51.

In the reign of 'Umar, the memorisation of the Qur'ān started with Ubayy b. Ka'b and 'Abdullāh b. Mas'ūd, and by that time the collection of it also began. As regards the commentary, it commenced with Ibn 'Abbās (d. 68/687) sometime after the reign of the Orthodox Caliphs.[62] By that time many non-Muslims had accepted Islam and so this need of rendering comments to writing was seriously felt, but it is to be regretted that many mediocre narrators ascribed their own comments to Ibn 'Abbās.[63]

Similarly, the meaning of *Qiṣāṣ* in the verse "*Qiṣāṣ* is prescribed to you in cases of the *Qatalā*" is taken by Shāh Walīyullāh as "equality" and not "retaliation" as given by many a commentator, and the word *qatalā* according to him means the murdered only. In this way he says that one would not be dragged either to the possibility of abrogation or committed to any forced explanation of the words "the woman for the woman". Here he has divided mankind into three classes. The first one includes the Muslims, and that is what is signified by the words "the free for the free," the second one consists of the non-Muslims and this is indicated by the words "the slave for the slave" and the third class relates to the two genera of mankind, male and female, and this is the meaning implied in the words "the woman for the woman". This recognition of equality among

62. Ibid., Vol. I, p. 51.

63. Maulānā 'Ubaidullāh Sindhī, *Qur'ān Pāk kā Muṭāla'ah Kaisey Kiyā Jā'ay.*

mankind is the very basis of the preservation of life.[64]

This shows that the explanation of the rarities of the Qur'ān is subject to independent reasoning.[65]

At the close of this chapter we once again repeat that Shāh Walīyullāh draws our attention to the study of the Qur'ān with meditation and to the acting upon its injunctions, and in so doing, to taking the life of the Prophet as an example.

During the days of the Companions it had become a matter of course, first, to read ten verses at the most, understand them fully and then translate them into action. When that was over, other ten verses were read, fully grasped and given practical shape. This is how those people approached the Qur'ān.[66]

An example of reading the Qur'ān with mind and thought applied together is found in the person of Ibn 'Umar who under the guidance of the Holy Prophet took eight years to finish the Chapter Baqarah. It was not merely reading with the tongue but acting on it as well.[67]

However, it may be remembered that the Qur'ān is not the scripture of simply knowledge by which the perfection of one single person is intended. But in addition to that, God took special care for the refor-

64. *Muṣaffā, Musawwā,* Vol. II, pp. 106-07 ; *al-Fauz-ul-Kabir*, p. 37. 'Abdullāh Yūsuf 'Alī has also translated *Qiṣāṣ* as equality. See his English translation of the Qur'ān, Vol. I, p. 70 (Sūrah al-Baqarah, verse 178).

65. *Al-Fauz-ul-Kabir* p. 37 :

و ازان جمله شرح غریب است - - - در اینجا نیز عقل را مدخل است
و اختلاف را گنجائش -

66. Commentary by Ibn Kathīr, Vol. I, p. 3.

67. *Al-Musawwā*, Vol. II, p. 312.

mation of all the people. Its example is like the example of the power of multiplying generation created in man, by which the reformation of the whole species is intended, even though it brings in its wake a perfection in that particular person, but by that also is intended the reformation of the person in such a way as to lead to the reformation of the species itself in whatever form it may be.[68]

In the opinion of Shāh Walīyullāh, the real science is one which meets the requirements of time and that science to him is the Holy Qur'ān only, as it is always apace with the time and ready to respond to its call.[69]

If anyone wishes to acquire the knowledge of the present age, then, according to Shāh Ṣāḥib, it is necessary for him to take the obvious meaning of the Qur'ān and keep away from interpretation as far as possible.[70]

Fatḥ-ur-Raḥmān is a living example of that reality, as, in spite of being too brief, it solves many a problem. If this Commentary and *Ḥujjatullāh-ul-Bāligha*h be prescribed for the higher course in the religious institutions, it will indeed be a great service to religion.[71]

68. *Al-Budūr-ul-Bāzighah*, p. 177.

69. *Tafhimāt*, Vol. II, p. 166 :

ان العلم الحق عندنا ما كان بمشائعة الحال و القرآن - - انما نزل بمشائعة الحال -

70. Ibid., Vol. I, p. 37 :

من أراد تحصيل هذه الدورة فعليه ان يقرأ القرآن بموضحه -

71. Maulānā 'Ubaidullāh Sindhī, *Shāh Walīyullāh Aur Un Kā Falsafah*, pp. 52-57.

Chapter II

THE TRADITION

IN the *Sharī'ah* after the Holy Qur'ān, the other great authority to rely upon is the Tradition. It is the foundation of the religious sciences and occupies a very high place among certain sciences.[1]

Shāh Walīyullāh realised fully that, for the restoration of a decadent community to its original seat of dignity and honour, it is necessary to revive the science of Tradition and dispel confusion from it wherever it appears. With this object in view he instituted an academy (*Dār-ul-Ḥadīth*), the first of its kind in the subcontinent, which was adequately developed by his worthy son Shāh 'Abd-ul-'Azīz after him.

He narrates: "When I found the theologians at variance and the Learned among them divided into sections, each one given to playing tricks in supporting the view of one's *Imām*, I turned to God in prayer to show me the right path through. Luckily I was given a hint to have a recourse to the *Muwaṭṭa'* of Imām Mālik, and then, later, I was convinced that at present no book on Jurisprudence is more authentic and trustworthy than that."[2]

1. Certain sciences, like mathematics, history and religious sciences which, when studied, lead one to certaintv and conviction.

2. *Muṣaffā* :

- - - و بیقین معلوم شد که امروز هیچ کتابی از کتب فقه أقوی از موطا نیست .

The thirst which Shāh Ṣāḥib had for the acquisition of the science of Tradition could not be quenched at Delhi. He, however, studied at the hands of Muḥammad Afdal of Sialkot, the celebrated traditionist of his time, some books like the *Mishkāt-ul-Maṣābīḥ*, *Shamā'il-un-Nabī* and a portion of *Saḥīḥ-ul-Bukhārī*, but all this was incomplete and far from being satisfactory.[3] He completed the study of this science and acquired proficiency in it at the hands of eminent scholars of Mecca and Medina when he visited those holy cities in 1143/1731.[4]

While giving lessons he always laid emphasis upon those points wherein both the Ḥanafī and Shāfi'ī schools were in agreement and avoided giving preference to one over the other. The adoption of this method resulted not only in broadening the outlook of the students but also created in them the spirit of tolerance and respect for the other schools of thought and their originators.

Traditions, as is well known, began to be put into writing one hundred years after the death of the Holy Prophet and their composition came to completion after an expiry of the second century. In 86/705 the Caliph Walīd appointed 'Umar b. 'Abd-ul-'Azīz as the governor of Medina, who gathered its scholars and entrusted to them the task of writing Traditions. This is how the foundation was laid. Until that time the only law to be consulted was the Holy Qur'ān.

3. Sayyid 'Abd-ul-Ḥayy al-Ḥasanī, *Nuzhat-ul-Khawāṭir wa Bahjat-ul-Masāmi' wa'n-Nawāẓir*, Vol. VI, p. 399.

4. *Insān-ul-'Ain fi Mashā'ikh-il-Ḥaramain.*

The main reason of the splitting up of Traditions into different kinds is due to their difference in the *Isnād* (ascription of a Tradition). Some were classed as *Mustafīḍ* (a Tradition vouched for by more than two Companions), some as *Hasan* (a Tradition of fair authority) and the others as *Mursal* (a Tradition with incomplete *Isnād*), etc. Consequently, it became necessary to examine and scrutinise thoroughly their validity, reliability and evidential value, which again inevitably necessitated the knowledge of the *Isnād*. As we have not seen the Prophet nor have we received anything directly from him, the preservation of *Isnād* is but indispensable for the survival of the *Sharī'ah*.[5]

It is for this very reason that the Caliph 'Umar, fearing lest the narrator may attribute false sayings to the Prophet, deliberately prevented people from indiscriminate narrations.

Classification. Bearing all these things in mind, Shāh Sāḥib has classified the Traditions. Thus, in the first class are included those Traditions which have been accepted at all counts as sound by the expert Traditionists, and adopted by the Jurists as an authority, such as the *Muwaṭṭa'* of Imām Mālik (94-179/713-795), *Ṣaḥīḥ* of Bukhārī (194-256/810-870) and *Ṣaḥīḥ* of Muslim (d. 261/875).

The second class consists of the *Jāmi'* of Tirmidhī (d. 279/892), the *Sunan* of Abū Dāwūd (d 275/888) and the *Sunan* of Nasā'ī (d. 303/915); while in the third class come those Traditions which, though they have

5. *Al-Irshād Ilā Muhimwāt 'Ilm-il-Isnād*,

been narrated by the ancients, no care was taken to determine their standard as to whether they were sound or unsound; like *Musnad* of Abū 'Alī, *Muṣannaf* of 'Abd-ur-Razzāq, *Musannaf* of Abū Bakr b. Abī Shaibah, and the works of Baihaqī and Ṭabarānī. The fourth class is inclusive of such Traditions which were not even heard of during the past, but were narrated very late, and as such they could not be trusted. For example, *Kitāb-ul-Ḍu'afā'* by Ibn Ḥabbān, *Kāmil* by Ibn 'Adī, the books of al-Khaṭīb and Ibn 'Asākir, etc. There are other works on the Traditions also, replete with good and bad, and they are not an authority to be accepted.

In a state of affairs like this it, therefore, becomes necessary to set a standard of testing the Traditions. Accordingly, the Traditions which are not covered by the first two classes should not be given equal weight and importance, however strong their authority (*sanad*) be, because if all the Traditions were to be brought under consideration, then it is quite likely that they become a cause for controversy. The innovators like Rāfidites and Mu'tazilites and some other misguided groups can with little effort find out some material from those records of the Traditions (belonging to the third and fourth classes) in support of their own crude beliefs. The procedure of making reference to the Traditions belonging to the third and fourth classes and quoting them as an authority is discounted and does not find favour with the learned Traditionists.[6]

6. *Ḥujjatullāh*, Vol. I, pp. 133-35; *Fimā yajib ḥifẓahū lin-nāẓir*; Shāh 'Abd-ul-'Azīz, *'Ujjalah Nāfi'ah*.

As regards the *Sunan* of Ibn Mājjah, it is really strange to note that its name does not occur anywhere in the works of Shāh Walīyullāh save in the *Izālat-ul-Khafā'* where he has discussed the appearance of Imām Mahdī. The perfect Jurists are, however, of the opinion that a Tradition which has been exclusively mentioned by it is either *Mauḍū'* (false) or *Ḍa'īf* (weak).[7]

This kind of classification of the Traditions has given a new life to the science of Tradition, as this way of approach towards the study of the Tradition has certainly closed the door of that kind of learning which is not based on research.[8]

It is, therefore, that Shāh Ṣāḥib says, somewhere, that there is one party which does not carry on an independent inquiry into the science of Tradition, nor has it ever learnt this science at the hands of competent teachers. Such a party follows the course of a copyist. This party indeed forms a sophistic group in the Prophet's community, as it neither held fast to the skirts of *Taqlīd* nor rightly chose the path of independent thinking. Such a party miserably failed in its attempt at clearing the difference in varying Traditions or effecting an agreement among them, and could not differentiate the sense implied in one Tradition from the one implied in the other and thereby lost itself in many a theological and scholas-

7. Maulānā 'Ubaidullāh Sindhī, Shāh Walīyullāh Number of *al-Furqān* (Bareilly, 1941).

8. Maulānā 'Ubaidullāh Sindhī, *Shāh Walīyullāh aur Un kā Falsafah*, pp. 97-120.

tic issue.[9]

Muwaṭṭa'. Shāh Walīyullāh (against the consensus of the *'Ulamā'*) has assigned the first position to the *Muwaṭṭa'* of Mālik which he considers the most correct record of Tráditions. For that he gives reasons:

(1) This is, however, an undeniable fact that the number of narrators who transmitted the Traditions mentioned in the *Muwaṭṭa'* hardly exceeds two; as such it is much easier to examine them critically and establish the validity of the *Isnād* of narrators.

(2) The majority of those narrators who are held trustworthy and dependable by the religious leaders of the Muslims (*A'immat-ul-Muslimīn*) belonged to Medina, the home of the *Sunnah*.

(3) What characterises *Muwāṭṭa'* is that wherever Imām Mālik has not been able to find out a Tradition in support of a certain problem, he adopts the practice of the people of Medina. For example, there he uses the words: "*al-amr-ul-ladhī lā ikhtilāf fīh.*" And by the practice of the people of Medina is meant that practice which continued as such, without a break, from the days of the Orthodox Caliphs. Naturally, such a kind of practice in itself is an independent authority. Anyhow, here a door has been left open for a research scholar, to carry on his research, to find out a Tradition, if any, about that problem.

(4) Both Imām Shāfi'i and Imām Muḥammad studied *Muwaṭṭa'* under Imām Mālik; and though they differed from him in the method of inference

9. *Qurrat-ul-'Ainain fi Tafḍil-ish-Shaikhain*, p. 177.

(*Istinbāṭ*), they had no difference with him so far as the soundness of the *Isnād* (chain of narrators) was concerned. All other books on the Traditions are in a way an exposition and an appendix of *Muwaṭṭa'*, considering that the additional *sanads* which have been brought in those books just lend support to those of *Muwaṭṭa'*.[10]

(5) This fact should also be borne in mind that when the Prophet migrated to Medina, the social movement of Islam assumed the shape of an independent institution there; and after his death, during the caliphate of the first three caliphs, it continued to remain the centre of Islamic movement And even after their reign when civil war broke out among the Muslims themselves and Ḥaḍrat 'Alī made Kūfah the centre of his political movement, and later on, when the Umayyads shifted their capital to Damascus, Medina continued to be the centre of Islam. This is the very reason why the fundamentals and the teachings of the complete system of the New Faith which came into existence through the influence of the Holy Qur'ān and the Practice of the Holy Prophet remained preserved with the people of Medina. Imām Mālik brought them all into his book *Muwaṭṭa'* and, as such, it should be treated as the foremost and the most authentic collection of both the Traditions and Jurisprudence.[11]

Imām Bukhārī, no doubt, took unusual care in

10. *Al-Muṣaffā*, Vol. I, p. 7.
11. Maulānā 'Ubaidullāh Sindhī, *Shāh Waliyullāh aur Unki Siyāsī Taḥrīk*, pp. 58-59.

sifting the Traditions and compiling the most authentic of them. He separated the valid from the invalid and retained only the reliable. He is held in high esteem for his having fixed strict rules to determine the trustworthiness of narrators (*Rāwīs*), and his book covers the whole field of *Fīqh*. God had indeed blessed him with extraordinary power of discernment. But his collection also appeared two hunded years after the Ḥijrah. Some scholars, says Shāh Ṣāḥib, do not accept his method, namely, of taking any of the two words capable of different meanings as an evidence for a problem (*mas'alah*).[12]

Shāh Sāḥib, realising the importance of *Muwaṭṭa'* and calling himself the promoter of its cause, is so anxious for its study that at one place, making no secret of his mind, he fervently appeals that, when the student is found fit and is capable to understand Arabic, he should be taught *Muwaṭṭa'*. He believes that it is the very foundation of the science of Tradition and its study is a great blessing.[13]

Laying further emphasis on its usefulness he remarks: "I am convinced for various reasons that today the door of *Ijtihād* (independent thinking on the derivation of religious laws from the Qur'ān and the Tradition) is completely closed save that one were to keep *Muwaṭṭa'* before oneself for consultation."[14]

12. *Maktūbāt, Bāb Ḥadith Bukhāri*:
بعض محققین آن را قبول نمی کنند مانند استدلال هریکی از دو محتمل لفظ برائی مسئله ۔

13. *Wasiyat-Nāmah.*
14. *Muṣaffā*, Vol. I, pp. 10-11.

In the Introduction it has already been pointed out that *Ḥujjatullāh-ul-Bālighah*, the *magnum opus*, is the unique production of Shāh Walīyullāh. He has given therein an exhaustive account of the science of Tradition and has unravelled the secrets underlying it. The book is so informative on this point that it won't be an exaggeration to call it a work of the Tradition. Shāh 'Abd-ul-'Azīz observes that, in explaining the mysteries implied in the science of Tradition, *Ḥujjatullāh-ul-Bālighah* is the best composition. No doubt, we have some specimens of the same in *Iḥyā'* of Ghazālī, and in the *al-Qawā'id-ul-Kubrā* of Shaikh 'Izz-ud-Dīn 'Abd-us-Salām ash-Shāmī, but in comparison to *Ḥujjatullah-ul-Bālighah* they are of much less value.[15]

Shāh Ṣāḥib himself has also made a bold claim about it.[16]

Explanation. Herein below is cited a couple of examples illustrating the truth of his claim:

(1) There is a Qur'ānic verse: "Think not of those who are slain in the path of God as dead; nay, they live finding their sustenance in the presence of their Lord."

The comments upon this verse as given by the Holy Prophet are as follows:

"The spirits of the martyrs are put into the crops of green birds which come down to the rivers of Paradise and eat of its fruit and take shelter in golden chandeliers suspended in the shadow of God's throne." [17]

Explaining this Tradition, Shāh Ṣāḥib says that

15. *Nuzhat-ul-Khawāṭir.* Vol. VI, p. 402. (Shaikh 'Izz-ud-Dīn was a great Shāfi'ī theologian and died in 660/1262.)

16. *As-Sirr-ul-Maktūm fi Asbāb Tadwin-il-'Ulūm*; *al-Juz'-u'l-Laṭif.*

17. *Sunan Abū Dāwūd, Bāb fi Fāḍl-ish-Shahādah.*

the man who is killed in the path of God carries with himself two qualities. One is his spirit (*Nasmah*) which by that time remains complete and full of the noble sciences he was engaged in during his lifetime, such as do not disappear from his heart. An example of such a martyr is like one who is overwhelmingly busy in his means of living, and in this state is taken by sleep. His case is quite different from that of him who died after a long and protracted illness, when his whole constitution changed, and he forgot much of the knowledge he was devoted to before.

The other quality of the martyr is that the Divine Mercy, which is always engaged in the establishment of the best order on the surface of the earth and with which the Holy Fold (*Ḥaẓīrat-ul-Quds*) and the angels nearest to God are replete and full, enshrouds and wraps him up. Now when the soul of this martyr, whose faculties both interior and exterior were actively working for the support of the true religion and the exaltation of the word of God and its propagation, quits the body, there opens up a wide passage between him and the Holy Fold until he finds himself inundated by blessings and happiness beyond bounds. His heart is infused and inspired by the Holy Fold and his reward consequently assumes the shape he had in mind. The combination of these two qualities, then, gives rise to many a wonderful thing; for example, he happens to see himself suspended in one or the other form upon the highest heaven and that is so because he now happens to be closely associated with the angels.

Another of these wonderful things is that he finds

himself in the shape of a green bird. The cause for his representation of the bird of this kind is that he is now being counted as one of the angels who are ever in flight, soaring and circling in the highest heaven. The nearest of any forms among all the animals for them to assume is that of the bird, which summarily reflects the properties and the predications (*aḥkām*) of the animals. The reason for the green colour seems to be its pleasing and delightful sight. His blisses and comforts will assume the form of various foods of Paradise just as the worldly blisses and comforts assume the shape of delicious dishes and fruits.[18]

(2) There is a Tradition that once the Holy Prophet asked Bilāl to tell him the act by which he preceded him in the entry to Paradise where he heard the thumping of his (Bilāl's) shoes.

Shāh Ṣāḥib here narrates that once, while he was giving his lesson, one of the students asked him to explain the significance of Bilāl's preceding the Prophet in entering the Paradise, when the latter excels all the prophets and mankind as a whole. This is in no way admissible that any man should surpass the Holy Prophet in any branch of excellence.

"I in my explanation," says Shāh Ṣāḥib, "told him that sleep means the representation of the picture in imagination. The mind of man is a repository of so many pictures, and when with all its presence it turns to any one of them, naturally the thought of others disappears. As an example, when you begin to think

18 *Ḥujjatullāh-ul-Bālighah*, Vol. II, pp. 172-73.

in your mind that you are a king, an absolute ruler, sitting on a throne with a crown on your head, your soldiers, ministers and attendants standing before you in lines (with reverence), and that you are pondering over the plans of war, at that time, the thought of your self as to how low and mean it is, just like others', will never come to you. But the moment you looked to yourself, the first state will stay no longer. The Holy Prophet in that sleep took his own pure self as one of the rest of mankind, and did not pay any heed whatsoever to his prophetic attribute, nor did he ever think of his having been the best of all mankind, and even the imaginative picture of that reality did not draw to him. In such a case Bilāl's going ahead of him due to his virtuous act is not surprising."[19]

As for the saying of the Prophet: "I heard, before my entering the Paradise, the thumping of your shoes," it points out to the fact that to remain with ablution all the time, and then to perform a portion of prayer after every ablution, is absolutely necessary for the achievement of the degree of *Iḥsān* (goodness), and only that man can keep up to it who has been blessed with a copious share of it; and the Prophet's saying: "What is that act by which you entered Paradise before me?" signifies his (Bilāl's) taking the lead in the degree of *Iḥsān*.

Explaining further, Shāh Ṣāḥib states that, in opposition to every acclivity of perfection, there is a declivity, an example of which is as follows: "Zaid,

19. *Sharḥ Tarājim Abwāb Ṣaḥiḥ-i'l-Bukhāri*, pp. 80-81.

for example, being a poet is also a mathematician. The time he thinks of his poetry and his high proficiency therein, he gets so much delighted that he completely forgets his being a mathematician; but the moment he thinks of his mathematics, his high qualifications and achievements therein, his thought of being a poet hardly occurs to him. The prophets generally have to deal with the common people, and the Ḥoly Prophet on that particular occasion looked to himself as one of them and in a state of his declivity saw Bilāl preceding him and from that he drew the conclusion that he (Bilāl) is firmly grounded in the field of *Iḥsān*."[20]

Practical Wisdom. Wherever he mentions a Tradition, he clearly manifests the practical wisdom (*ḥikmat-i-'amalī*) contained therein. This inevitably results in the realisation of the importance of the action rather than that of the thought, and the reader is unusually impressed.

Practical wisdom is a branch of a science which deals with the realities of the existing things, and probes deep into them in order that the good of this world and of the world to come be achieved. It is of three kinds.

(1) That which relates to the individual good of man, termed as civilisation (good breeding) and ethical philosophy.

(2) That which concerns the good of a party whose members live together in some place, and it is called the household economy.

20. *Ḥujjatullāh-ul-Bālighah*, Vol. II, pp. 19-20.

(3) That which pertains to the good and well-being of a community settled in a big town with all its members living in peace and amity with each other, and this is called civic economy (art of government).[21]

The principle under which Shāh Ṣāḥib has effected the gradation of the Traditions leaves no scope for any kind of clash among them ; and if at all some clash appears somewhere, it can be overcome very easily.

Agreement. In the elimination of difference from the seemingly conflicting Traditions, Shāh Walīyullāh was unquestionably a past master and holds a unique position, and, in this respect, his selfless services to religion will be remembered for ever.[22]

To give preference to one Tradition over the other, no doubt, satisfies the presumption (*Ẓann*), but effecting of an agreement between the two certainly leads to conviction, and Shāh Sāhib stands unparalleled in this art. Here below are given some examples demonstrative of his wisdom and skilfulness in bringing reconciliation between the Traditions in conflict, bearing testimony to the vastness of his knowledge which he had of the science of Tradition.

(1) There is a Tradition, reporting the Prophet to have said that the caliphate after him would last for thirty years. Again, there is another Tradition wherein he has said that the handmill of Islam would continue moving for thirty-five years. Apparently there is a contradiction between the two Traditions.

Shāh Ṣāḥib here has successfully tried to show that

21. *As-Sirr-ul-Maktūm fī Asbāb Tadwīn-i'l-'Ulūm* ; *al-Juz'-ul-Laṭīf.*
22. *Ath-Thaqāfat-ul-Islāmiyyah fi'l-Hind*, p. 287.

no contradiction whatsoever exists between them. He in his explanation states that if ten years of the Holy Prophet's life prior to Hijrah be deducted from thirty-five years, the number will be reduced to twenty-five only.

Now, if we include the Caliph 'Alī among other caliphs because of his valuable services done to Islam and of his being the best of all in his time, the period of caliphate comes to thirty years. But in case we do not count him among them on the ground that there was no political stability in his times and many a revolt and rebellion took place during his days, and that the caliphate in particular ended with the death of 'Uthmān, then its duration comes up to twenty-five years.[23]

Qarn. It is, therefore, necessary to remove the misunderstanding likely to crop up here. The Prophet had said, "The best age (*Qarn*) is that of mine, then of those who will come after my age and then of those who will come after their age."

By the first age is generally meant the age of the Holy Prophet and of the Orthodox Caliphs. By the second and third is meant the age of the immediate followers of the Companions and of those who followed the immediate followers.

In the opinion of Shāh Walīyullāh, this interpretation of the *Qarn* is not correct. He gives his own explanation and in support of it quotes many a Tradition. He explains that the first *Qarn* (age) is that which

23. *Izālat-ul-Khafā' 'an-Khilāfat-ul-Khulafā'*, Vol. I, p. 29; *Qurrat-ul-'Ainain fi Tafḍil-ish-Shaikhain*, p. 143.

begins with the Hijrah of the Holy Prophet and ends with his death. The second *Qarn* starts with the caliphate of Abū Bakr and terminates with the death of 'Umar, while the period of 'Uthmān's caliphate be taken as the third *Qarn*. In this way every *Qarn* is of twelve years approximately; and there are so many Traditions from which it is learnt that the handmill of Islam will move for thirty-five, thirty-six or thirty-seven years.

The word *Qarn* etymologically signifies equality in age or persons close to each other in their ages. In its literal meaning it also signifies persons near to one another in rulership and caliphate. But when the caliph changed, his ministers and chiefs also changed and the officers of the army also changed as happened in the days of 'Alī, the *Qarn* would be taken as having changed.

According to Shāh Ṣāḥib, all the Traditions despite their difference in wording concurrently point towards the same purpose, namely, the period as mentioned before. During that period in particular, Islam and its rule gained domination and power in the proper sense of the word.[24]

(2) There is a saying of the Prophet: "The first army of my community which will invade the country of Caesar is forgiven."

On the basis of this saying, some people find justification for the forgiveness of Yazīd. It is so because Yazīd was not only one of the army personnel, but

24. *Izālat-ul-Khafā' 'an Khilāfat-ul-Khulafā'*, Vol. I, pp. 75, 121.

he was the chief commander of it, a fact amply testified by history. On the other side, there are Traditions in condemnation of those who remain in pursuit of bringing insult and injury to the family of the Prophet.

These conflicting Traditions, he says, can be reconciled in this way, if we say that Yazīd's sins committed before that military expedition were forgiven on account of his participation in that, because *Jihād* (Holy War) is the expiation of the sins, and the expiation relates to the obliteration of the past sins and not of the future ones. As for the sins which he committed after that war, namely, the murder of Imām Ḥusain, devastation of Medina, and addiction to wine-drinking, etc., are matters to be taken as pending with God for decision.[25]

(3) There is a Tradition, according to which the Prophet has said: "When you see the caliphate has been shifted to Syria, you should know that serious situations and frightful events are soon to take place, and the Judgment Day is near." According to another Tradition, he is stated to have said: "The time is approaching fast when you would be the masters of large armies. One army would be in Syria, the other in Yemen and the third in Iraq." When Ibn Ḥawālah requested the Prophet to advise him as to which of the armies he would like him to join if he be living by that time, the Prophet told him to stay in Syria, saying: "It is a land liked by God, and He rehabilitates

25. *Sharḥ Tarājim Abwāb Ṣaḥīḥ-i'l-Bukhārī*, p. 96.

there those whom He likes."

This clash can be averted if "we [Shāh Ṣāḥib] say that the Syrians were not entitled to caliphate on account of their personal qualities, but the caliphate somehow went to their lot and they were supported by God in their efforts to carry on the Holy War (*Jihād*). Accordingly, where there is a mention of their wickedness, it refers to their personal qualities and where there is a mention of their goodness, it has reference to their state politics in which they were undoubtedly expert."[26]

(4) As regards the thigh, all the four Imāms are not in agreement as to whether it is obligatory to cover it or not. Both Imām Abū Hanīfah and Shāfi'ī declare it to be obligatory, while there is Imām Mālik who holds the opposite view. There are of course Traditions in support of both these views, but from the point of transmission-chain (narration), the view of Imām Mālik is weightier and stronger.[27]

Here Shāh Ṣāḥib says that the way to remove their difference and bring about *rapprochement* is this that the Traditions, according to which the revealing of the thigh is not counted as an immodesty, should be taken to refer to the thigh of a man, in relation to those who visit him often and are his confidants, but the same be regarded as an immodesty in relation to those who are not so familiar and social with him and visit him sparingly. For them, looking at the open thigh is disallowed.

26. *Izālat-ul-Khafā'*, Vol. I, p. 155.
27. *Sharḥ Tarājim Abwāb Ṣaḥīḥ-i'l-Bukhārī*, pp. 39-40.

The above agreement is seconded and aptly illustrated by the occasion on which 'Uthmān came to the Holy Prophet when the latter's thigh lay uncovered. The time 'Uthmān appeared, the Prophet hurriedly covered up his thigh while it lay uncovered in the presence of Abū Bakr and 'Umar, because they were his frequent visitors.

As for Imām Mālik's permission to the labourers and the workers to keep their thighs open during prayer, it is also correct, and is corroborated by a number of Traditions. The Holy Prophet, as is well known, on no occasion compelled the labour class to cover up their thighs up to their knees in prayers.

Here we have a general rule, namely, that the Holy Prophet has clearly explained two aspects of prayer. One is the prayer of the special and the other is that of the common people. There are many such instances wherein the Prophet allowed certain things in one case and disallowed them in the other. If this rule is brought into consideration, then the apparent opposition among the Traditions can on many occasions be easily removed.[28]

The examples mentioned above are a clear indication of Shāh Ṣāḥib's ability and tactfulness in bringing harmony between the Traditions at variance.

In short, Shāh Ṣāḥib's approach towards the study of the *Ḥadīth* is that the famous and celebrated books should be read as, for example, *Muwaṭṭa'*, *Ṣaḥīḥ Bukhārī*, *Ṣaḥīḥ Muslim*, *Sunan* of Abū Dāwūd, and *Jāmi'*

28. Ibid.

of Tirmidhī, because the validity of these books is well established and is above question. The complete study of these books, he says, can be gained in a short time, and this for the student of *Ḥadīth* is the most precious thing these days.[29]

The valuable service which Shāh Walīyullāh has done to the science of Tradition will never be forgotten by the inhabitants of the Indo-Pakistan subcontinent.[30]

29. *Tafhimāt*, Vol. I, p. 156.
30. *Ath-Thaqāfat-ul-Islāmiyyah fi'l-Hind*, p. 139.

Chapter III

THE JURISPRUDENCE

AFTER the Qur'ān and the Tradition, the third source of religious information is the Jurisprudence (*Fiqh*). It deals with worships, obligations, modes of conduct, mutual transactions, home affairs and state politics. This science was not written during the lifetime of the Holy Prophet, nor was there raised any question of critical nature about religious matters those days. As a matter of fact, the Companions never used to put too many questions to the Holy Prophet, and throughout his life asked him only eleven questions which were already there in the Holy Qur'ān.[1]

All the books and collections of Jurisprudence are new works which appeared much later. Expression of different views, giving decision on the strength of one man's religious opinion, and to adopt and rely upon it was not the practice current among people in the first two centuries.[2]

In the third century, it, however, became a fashion of the day to adopt and follow the definite school of thought of one particular *Mujtahid* (independent interpreter of the canon law), and to do so was the necessity of times.

1. *Al-Inṣāf fi Bayān Sabab-i'l-Ikhtilāf.*
2. Ibid.

With the beginning of the fourth century, the absolute (*Muṭlaq*) *Mujtahid* disappeared, while the office of the related *Mujtahid* (*al-Mujtahid al-Muntasib*), however, will continue to be occupied right up to the Judgment Day. *Ijtihād* of this kind is a general duty (*farḍ-i-kifāyah*) which, if given up at any time, will involve the whole community in sin.

After the expiry of the fourth century, the differences of opinion in relation to certain points of Jurisprudence multiplied, and the imitation of a particular *Imām* firmly settled in the hearts of men. The cause of all this was the disagreement and quarrels among the Jurists themselves. Thereafter, every century that followed brought in an ever-increasing number of disputes and conflicts among the religious leaders, and blind imitation gained an added strength. People ceased to trust each other and gave up thinking and meditating upon religion.[3]

Ijtihād. New problems are taking place in increasing number day by day, so it is necessary to understand the Divine injunctions concerning them. Whatever has been said and done before is not sufficient and, apart from that, there are many differences about that also. Those differences again cannot be resolved unless they are considered in the light of evidences. And it is hardly possible to trace those evidences to their original authors. When things stand as such, there is no other way out, but to examine the problems on the basis of independent thinking

3. Ibid.

(*Ijtihād*).[4]

Ijtihād as a matter of fact is the only instrument left with us for solving the problems emerging out in the swiftly changing conditions of the modern times.

Shāh Walīyullāh has condemned blind imitation outright. He has tried to break the extreme rigidity of the learned (*'Ulamā'*) which they observed in the imitation, and wanted to change it by an independent interpretation. This is the reason why he insisted upon the study and research in the science of Tradition.[5]

Shāh Ṣāḥib, therefore, started a vigorous campaign against innovations and superstitions of the worst type in his days, and tried to preserve and maintain the purity of Islam. This campaign, after him, was relentlessly carried on by his grandson Shāh Ismā'īl Shahīd.

It will, however, be absolutely wrong to think that Shāh Walīyullāh had completely thrown off the rope of imitation from himself. Truly, imitation did not suit his nature, but expediency lay in his adherence to it.[6]

4. *Muṣaffā*, Vol. I, p. II :

اجتهاد در هر عصر فرض بالکفایه است و مراد از اجتهاد اینجا نه اجتهاد مستقل است مثل اجتهاد شافعی ـ ـ ـ مسائل کثیر الوقوع غیر محصور اند ـ ـ ـ و آنچه مسطور شده است نیز غیر کافی و در آنها اختلاف بسیار ـ ـ ـ صرف احادیث جمیع احکام را کفایت نمی کند ـ

5. *Tafhimāt*, Vol. I, pp. 209-10.

6. *Fuyūḍ-ul-Ḥaramain*, Mashhad, p. 33.

The betterment of the common people, he says, lies in their following the four schools of thought; and it would be suicidal to rely upon the corrupt theologians (*'Ulamā' sū'*), particularly in this later age, wherein loyalty is no more cared for.[7]

If a learned man were to find truth with the other school of thought, then, merely for the sake of his obedience to the school of his *Imām*, he should not reject it, as this amounts to a flagrant violation of the truth.[8]

Shāh Walīyullāh fervently desired to see an end of all the disputes between the four schools of thought, and in this direction he played an important role. He actually settled their differences, and successfully worked for their agreement. His argument is that at present Ḥanafī and Shāfi'ī schools are the most famous, their works are numerous and they both command the maximum following, and the right course in conformity with the Divine Will requires that both be amalgamated. After that whatever be found in agreement with that unified school should be accepted and the rest, lacking in its original source, be rejected outright. In this respect he says that the *Muwaṭṭa'* of Imām Mālik can faithfully perform the duty of an arbitrator, as it provides the basis for the removal of mutual differences. The Traditions cited therein are the most authentic, and without consulting it the door of *Ijtihād* is practically

7. *Al-'Iqd-ul-Jīd fī Aḥkām-i'l-Ijtihād wa't-Taqlīd*, p. 31.
8. *Tafhīmāt*, Vol. I, p. 211.

closed.[9]

Ḥanafī School. In the Indo-Pakistan subcontinent Hanafī religion gained so much currency and popular support that with the Muslims it represented a true copy of Islam. For them, it had indeed become their national religion. Thus, if any reformer is to appear there at any time, he will have to go by the Ḥanafī school of thought. This is the only course left for him to carry his missionary work successfully, otherwise his mission will fail. This is why he was advised intuitively to give up opposition to the bye-laws of the Ḥanafī school in his country.[10]

Shāh Ṣāḥib himself used to act according to the Hanafī school of thought and preferred it to others, as it bears considerable resemblance with the other schools. Besides, from the jurisprudence point of view, namely, in determining the validity or otherwise of a certain issue, it enjoys pre-eminence over the rest. That point of jurisprudence is that the views of Abū Hanīfah and his two companions Abū Yūsuf and Muḥammad should be brought into consideration and then whosoever's view be found nearest to the Tradition should be accepted. Such procedure aimed at bring-

9. Ibid., Vol. I, pp 211-12; *al-Muṣaffā*, Vol. I, p. 11:

و آنکه گفتیم که امروز طریق اجتهاد مسدود است الا ازین جهت (که موطا را پیش نگیرد) بسبب آن است که صرف احادیث جمیع احکام را کفایت نمی کند لابد است از آثار صحابه و تابعین و حالاً هیچ کتابی که مخدوم باشد و نظر مجتهدانه در آن کرده باشد طبقة بعد طبقة غیر موطا نیست ۔

10. *Fuyūḍ-ul-Ḥaramain*, Mashhad, p. 33.

ing agreement between Tradition and Jurisprudence is indeed of far-reaching consequences.[11]

The course Shāh Walīyullāh has chosen in Jurisprudence is correct both in principle and in consequence, but his course is specially meant for those who have the aptitude for investigation and research and, in addition to that, the adoption of such a course should not in any way be the cause of a rift in the community.[12]

Here it is worth noting that, on the one side, Shāh Sāhib's father and uncle were Hanafites, while on the other side Shaikh Abū Ṭāhir and his father Shaikh Ibrāhīm Kurdī were the followers of the Shāfi'ī school of thought. Naturally, when Shāh Ṣāḥib benefited from both, he after thorough study and deep thinking found that both these schools were basically similar. Looking, therefore, at the conditions prevalent in his time, he remained the follower of the Hanafī school, and held the Shāfi'ī school also in high esteem. In practice he was a Ḥanafite but in theory and teaching he was both Ḥanafite and Shāfi'ite.[13]

Shāfi'ī School. It was indeed very wise on the part of Shāh Walīyullāh to have thought of the simultaneous study of both the Ḥanafī and Shāfi'ī schools as essential. The reason is obvious, as both these schools form the nucleus of religious laws. In fact, they play the constructive role in the structure of religious science. What adds to the fame and populari-

11. Ibid., pp. 19, 46.
12. Ibid., p. 10.
13. *Ilhām-ur-Raḥmān*, p. 332.

ty of the Shāfi'ī school is that there has appeared in it a large number of independent interpreters, Jurists, commentators, dialecticians and Traditionists. The basis of that school is the *Muwaṭṭa'* of Imām Mālik which is acknowledged as one nearest to the Tradition.[14]

There is of course no denying the fact that he gave preference to some points of the Shāfi'ī school, but he was fully aware of the attractiveness, simplicity and the ever-increasing popularity of the Hanafī school. He was indeed a loyal follower of it as it was to the taste of the non-Arabs and suited their conditions best.

Cause of Difference. In his *Inṣāf* Shāh Sāhib cites a few examples of certain questions about the original sources of which there is many a misunderstanding. In reality, this misunderstanding is the fountainhead of all the existing differences. They are summarised as follows.

(1) Many people are under the wrong impression that all the consequences of principles (*Tafrī'āt*) found in voluminous books in the treatment of decisions of sacred law are the sayings of Imām Abū Ḥanīfah and his two companions. But here they do not make a difference between their actual sayings and those which were subsequently deduced after having been brought into consideration their narrators and their legal decisions. They take the wording "according to the deduction (*Takhrīj*) of al-Karkhī is this" and

14. *Al-Khair-ul-Kathir*, p. 124 ; *al-Inṣāf*, p. 80.

"according to the deduction of *aṭ-Ṭaḥāwī* is this," as having no meaning.[15]

Unfortunately, they fail to recognise a distinction between "Abū Ḥanīfah has said like this" and "according to the Ḥanafī school, the reply to the question is this." They do not listen to what Ibn-ul-Humām and Ibn-un-Nujaim, the foremost among the Ḥanafites, have declared, that the question of "ten into ten" and that of the condition for the performance of ablution with sand (*tayammum*) are not from the sayings of Abū Ḥanīfah.[16]

Similarly, some persons are under the illusion that the foundation of the Ḥanafī school is based on polemics, as contained in books like *al-Mabsūṭ*, *al-Hidāyah* and *at-Tabyīn*. This is absolutely wrong. On the contrary, the Mu'tazilites were the first to start with this art of ecclesiastical controversies. Then those who came after chose their path, with the hope that it would make the learners more intelligent and broad-minded, but this hope of theirs did not materialise. Instead, it rendered them dull and prejudiced.

(2) Again, there are some who think that the basis of difference between Abū Hanīfah and Shāfi'ī is the principles enunciated by Bazdawī in his books; but, in fact, many of such principles have never been

15. Abu'l-Ḥasan, 'Ubaidullāh b. al-Ḥasan, al-Karkhī, was the famous theologian of Iraq. He died in 346/957.

Aḥmad b. Muḥammad Ṭaḥāwī studied Shāfi'ī Jurisprudence in the beginning, but later on he changed for the Ḥanafī school of thought. He wrote books on *Ḥadith* and *Fiqh* and died in 321/933.

16. *Tafhimāt*, Vol. II, p. 135. (Zain b. Ibrāhīm, known as Ibn-un-Nujaim was a reputed Ḥanafī theologian. He died in 970/1562.

mentioned by them. They, on the contrary, have been framed much later in the light of their speeches and decisions.[17]

As an illustration, Shāh Ṣāḥib cites a few examples of the principles of Jurisprudence, which the latter ones had only inferred from the speeches of the former ones, while no such speeches have ever been authoritatively narrated of them (Abū Hanīfah and his companions).

Principles. (1) *Khāṣṣ* (definite) by itself is abundantly clear and explanatory, and needs no comment.

(2) Like *khāṣṣ*, *'āmm* (indefinite) is also decisive.

(3) The tenor of condition (*mafhūm-i-sharṭ*) and that of attribute (*mafhūm-i-waṣf*) is out of consideration.

(4) If a narration by a person other than a jurist be found clashing with both the principle and the analogy, then it is not necessary to practise.[18]

These are some of the principles of Jurisprudence deduced from the speeches of the earlier *Imāms*, but there is no evidence whatsoever to prove their narration by Abū Hanīfah and his companions. Herein below their general principles mentioned above are being examined one by one.

(1) Their principle that the word *khāṣṣ* is clear and self-explanatory and does not need any com-

17. Shaikh-ul-Islām 'Alī b. Muḥammad al-Bazdawī is reckoned as the *Imām* of Ḥanafī scholars. He died in 482/1089 and has left many valuable works behind.

18. *Ḥujjatullāh-ul-Bālighah*, Vol. II, p. 111.

ments has actually been taken from the practice of the earlier ones, who on the basis of the verse "Prostrate and bow"[19] had prescribed only "bowing and prostrating" as obligatory in prayer but not the resting; while on the other hand there was a Tradition to the effect that the prayer of a man becomes nullified unless he holds his back straight both when he bows and prostrates.

The way the ancients adopted in this particular case gave a clue to the latter ones to form a general rule, but in many cases of similar nature, it has been recklessly violated by them. In the verse "Wipe your head,"[20] for example, there is the order of wiping the head only, and no limit of wiping is set. The word "wipe" is *Khāṣṣ*. According to the above-mentioned principle, the decision of general wiping of the head should have been given, but here the Ḥanafites do not pay full regard to their original principle, and on the strength of a Tradition, wherein the Prophet is reported to have performed the wiping of his forehead, have fixed one-fourth of the head for wiping. Now, here the question arises as to why these comments were appended to one which was already definite and self-explanatory.

(2) With regard to the reading in prayer, the Qur'ānic words are: "Read from the Qur'ān as much as is easy."[21] *Mātayassar* demands that, howsoever much and from wherever the Qur'ān is read, the

19. Sūrah al-Ḥajj, verse 77.
20. Sūrah al-Mā'idah, verse 6.
21. Sūrah al-Muzzammil, verse 20.

prayer would be valid and the Tradition "No prayer but with Fātiḥah" obviously requires its reading as obligatory. There the ancients, however, admitted the general application of the verse intact, but, refusing to acknowledge the Tradition of its particularisation, gave decision to the effect that the reading of Fātiḥah is not obligatory.

In like manner, the successors deduced from some of the sayings of their predecessors a general principle, namely, the *'āmm* (indefinite) is definite and independent in its significance, and its generality is not capable of any particularisation. According to that principle, the general application of the verse "Whatever *hadī* (animal for sacrifice) be easily available"[22] would also have been accepted as decisive, because therein the word "*Famastaisar*" is *'āmm* and, as such, its intended meaning also would have been taken in the general sense. But here, again, the Ḥanafites particularise it with a Tradition, and say that for *hadī* there should be an animal bigger than the goat. Now here, where remains the decisiveness of the indefinite like that of the definite?

(3) Again, "the tenor of condition and the attribute deserves no consideration". This means that, if a decision is given on a certain occasion, then in the application of that given decision, the conditions and the special circumstances of that occasion would not be taken into consideration. This rule has actually been taken from that course of the ancients which

22. Sūrah al-Baqarah, verse 196.

they had adopted in relation to the verse "If any of you have not the means to marry a free woman. . . ." Here, the outward of the verse gives meaning to the effect that, if a man has no means to marry a free woman, then he can marry a slave-woman. But, without recognising the condition of the lack of means, they gave permission to one with means to marry the slave-woman. The above principle has been inferred from that decision of theirs. But in the case of camel-tax these very persons have broken that rule. The wording of the text is "on the camels pasturing by themselves, tax is prescribed". The very same condition is mentioned here.

In accordance with the above principle, the tax should have been levied both on camels pasturing by themselves and on those not pasturing by themselves, and the meaning implied in the word *sā'imah* should not have been restricted. But in contravention of the accepted principle, the tax was prescribed only on the camels pasturing by themselves.[23]

(4) As regards the Tradition of *Muṣarrāt* (a sheep left unmilked in order that the milk may increase), the moderns, on the strength of the stand taken by the ancients, formulated a general principle that if a person other than the jurist happened to be the narrator of a Tradition in clash with analogy, then that Tradition would not be practicable by necessity. But these very founders of this principle

23. *Sā'imah*, camels, goats and the like, which live during the greater part of the year upon pasture. Sūrah an-Nisā', verse 25.

considered as necessary to practise the Tradition pertaining to *qahqahah* (loud laughter) in prayer, which is not only against analogy but has also been narrated by a person other than a jurist, and have given decision to the effect that with loud laughter in prayer, both the prayer and the ablution become null and void. But so far no intrinsic relationship between ablution and loud laughter has been conceived.

There are, however, many such examples which, on account of length, are to be omitted ; if a man does not carry a proper research and investigation he will not be benefited even by a lengthy discourse.[24]

From the above criticism it would be wrong to conclude that with Shāh Walīyullāh, the Ḥanafī school did not enjoy that esteem and consideration which was due to it. Of course, there is no denying the fact that he gave preference to some points of the Shāfi'ī school, but he, at the same time, was fully aware of the attractiveness, simplicity and the ever-increasing popularity of the Ḥanafī school. He was indeed a faithful follower of it, as it was to the taste of the non-Arabs who were more civilised and suited their condition best. The Arabs, on the contrary, lived more or less a bedouin life, and, as such, the *fiqh* of the other three *Imāms* proved useful for them.

Shāh Sāhib, however, tenaciously, sticks to the obvious meaning of the Book (Qur'ān) and the Tradition, and avoids as far as possible from indulging in the personal opinion (*rā'i*), as this in turn, he

24. *Ḥujjatullāh ul-Bālighah*, Vol. I, pp. 157-61.

says, gives rise to a new law (*Sharī'ah*). For example, the condition of one mile which the Ḥanafites have fixed in the verse: "If you do not find water . . ." is also the outcome of their personal opinion, and is not, in reality, the *madhhab* of Abū Ḥanīfah.[25]

Agreement. We have mentioned before that the valuable contribution of Shāh Walīyullāh is to bring about an agreement between the differing Traditions, and to transform their apparent heterogeneity into homogeneity. Indeed, he, in this art, is an expert, *par excellence.* Here below are given a few conflicting points of Jurisprudence and the manner he has effected harmony among them.

(1) There are varying reports with regard to the reading of the Qur'ān (by a follower) behind an *Imām* (leader in prayer). According to one, when once 'Umar was asked about it, he had replied in the affirmative. And when questioned what he would do in case he himself happened to be the *Imām*, there also he ratified his earlier reply. Again, when asked what would be his course if he happened to be reading (the Qur'ān in prayer) loudly, he also replied affirmatively. The Kūfian reports, on the other hand, are just the opposite and show that he had disallowed the reading (by a follower) behind an *Imām*.

Shāh Walīyullāh states that both these state-

25. *Al-Inṣāf* p. 91 ; Ibn Khaldūn, *Muqaddimah*, p. 449 ; *al-Muṣaffā*, Vol. I, pp. 27-28 :

و تحدید بمیل تقدیر برأی است و دل ما از تقدیر برأی در غایت قلق
است زیراکه تشریعی جدید می شود ـ

Sūrah al-Mā'idah, verse 6.

ments can be reconciled. The reading of the follower usually conflicts with that of the *Imām* and *vice versa.* In prayer, however, the concentration of thought upon God is desired. Now, if a man can withstand that conflict undisturbed, he may read behind his *Imām*, but he who is unable to do so should give up reading.[26]

(2) About the use of scent while in Pilgrim's garb, during Pilgrimage, Abū Bakr on the authority of Zaid b. Aslam, and he on the authority of his father narrated that, when once 'Umar felt the smell of scent at Dhul-Ḥulaifah, he inquired from whom it came. Mu'āwīyah replied, "It is with me and it has been applied to me by Umm Ḥabībah, and she has administered an oath to me not to wash it off." Hearing this, 'Umar ordered him to go back and get it washed by her which he actually did.[27]

This same report has again been seconded by Abū Bakr, who on the authority of Ibn 'Umar narrated that when 'Umar felt the smell of scent, he reprimanded its user. Mu'āwīyah, who had used it went back and got his scent-applied scarf properly washed.

Here Shāh Ṣāḥib says that the Jurists have not considered the Tradition narrated by 'Ā'ishah, wherein she is reported to have said: "I felt the smell of the scent from the parting line of the head of the Holy Prophet even after three days of his remaining in

26. *Izālat ul-Khafā'*, Vol. II, p. 93.

27. Dhul-Ḥulaifah is the *Miqāt* for the people of Medina. Here they will have to put on the Pilgrim's garb before proceeding to Mecca.

Iḥrām."

An agreement between the two is possible in this way, if we say that the use of scent to the body in *Iḥrām* is allowable, but its use on the clothes is forbidden. It is so because the dirtiness of the body takes away the scent soon, against that of the clothes where it lasts longer.[28]

In the art of harmonising the seemingly differing reports, Shāh Walīyullāh stands unrivalled. In fact, the explanation of the law which he is giving, if considered dispassionately, allows no scope for controversies, and the differences between the various schools of thought cease to exist. It is, therefore, that he is justified in his claiming himself to be the master in this art.[29]

There is absolutely no exaggeration in his assertion that he is like Ibn 'Abbās in the knowledge of the science of Law.[30]

Ijmā'. The '*Ijmā*' (consensus of the '*Ulamā*') is also an authority and an evidence for the understanding of the *Sharī'ah*. Shāh Sāhib, while making a reference to it, has already said that the Traditions alone do not suffice the requirements of the changing times. It had been the practice of the Companions, he says, that whenever they found any new problem having cropped up the answer of which they could not get from the Qur'ān or the Tradition, they used to sit together at

28. *Izālat-ul-Khafā'*, Vol. II, pp. 103-04.
29. *Tafhimāt*, Vol. I, pp. 82-83.
30. Ibid., Vol. II, p. 26 :

• انا ابن عباس من حيث فقاهتى فى الدين -

one place, and take a unanimous decision about it. Investigation has shown that up to the days of 'Uthmān, no discrepancy in the problem of Jurisprudence ever arose.[31]

In case a controversy took place on some occasion, the people referred the matter to their caliph, who after consultation gave a decision which invariably assumed the shape of the consensus. After the murder of 'Uthmān, every Jurisconsult began to give decision independently, and this is how the controversies in religious matters rose and multiplied.[32]

Ijmā' does not mean the unanimous opinion of all the learned the world over on a certain point without any dissension whatsoever. Such a case has never happened and can never happen. By *Ijmā'* is meant a decision which a caliph takes after consultation with the scholars and the doctors of law or even without their consultation, and that decision taken was so executed that the people throughout the country started acting upon it. Referring to the authenticity of this kind of *Ijmā'*, the Holy Prophet has said: "It is your duty to follow my practice and the practice of my Caliphs."[33]

The meaning of *Ijmā'* is the decision taken by the majority of religious thinkers, scholars and leaders of different places. Examples of such kind of *Ijmā'* are found in problems which were settled during the days

31. *Izālat-ul-Khafā'*, Vol. I, p. 283 :

اجاع امت در غیر زمان خلفاء ثلاثة متحقق نشده ۔

32. Ibid.

33. Ibid., p. 26.

of 'Umar. Decision taken by a large number of the learned, the scholars of Mecca and Medina and the Orthodox Caliphs also comes within the definition of *Ijmā'*.[34]

Ijmā' does not mean that a man without having made any reference to the *Sharī'ah* took a particular decision or adopted a certain view merely from the point of expediency, and the others supported it by chance. An *Ijmā'* which has not the backing of the Qur'ān and the Tradition and is not inferred from them both is not trustworthy.[35]

Following are the observations made by Maulānā 'Ubaidullāh Sindhī on the significance of *Ijmā'*:

"If a party, which rules according to the basic principles of the Qur'ān, takes a unanimous decision or if the majority supports the decision taken, it is also called an *Ijmā'*. This kind of *Ijmā'* can take place at all times. The only condition is that the party taking such a decision should be the follower of goodness and virtue. *Ijmā'* is not an independent principle of the religion. It is the name of the unanimous opinion of the party which works for the establishment of the Qur'ānic rule. In these days, for example, if the central Government were to take a certain decision, it would also be termed as *Ijmā'*. There seems to be no other way out but to accept such decision as an authority of the *Sharī'ah* itself, as without doing so no political movement in the world could work with success."[36]

'Umar's Role. In the knowledge of Jurisprudence, 'Umar was most advanced and better acquainted than others, and the services rendered by him in this

34. Ibid., p. 311 ; Vol. II, p. 85.

35. *Ḥujjatullāh-ul-Bāligha*, Vol. I, p. 121 ; *Izālat-ul-Khafā'*, Vol. I, p. 56.

36. *Shāh Waliyullāh aur Un kā Falsafah*, pp. 89-91.

field towards the community can never be forgotten. The points unanimously decided during his days were indeed the weightiest and the most reliable. A case which is disposed of with the unanimous consent of the community resembles most to the teachings of the prophets. The reason is that a conclusive decision on many problems of Jurisprudence can never be arrived at without *Ijmā'*. Again, the unanimity of the community cannot be achieved except through *Ijmā'*, and in the community nothing is so important and essential as the unanimity. The Prophet is also reported to have said: "My people will never agree upon an error." [37]

The points which remained unsolved in the lifetime of the Holy Prophet and in the reign of Abū Bakr and continued to be controversial were examined afresh during the days of 'Umar and a unanimous opinion was taken about them. Whatever remained unsettled will continue to be under dispute until the Judgment Day, and no agreement about it can ever be reached.[38]

It was indeed a procedure and a policy of Abū Bakr and 'Umar to search for the solution of a matter when referred to in the Qur'ān and the Tradition. If they could not have had a solution from either of them, then they all used to meet together

37. Abū Dāwūd, Tirmidhī.

38. *Qurrat-ul-'Ainain fī Tafḍīl-ish-Shaikhain*, pp. 59-60:

و اقوی مسائل فقهیه اجماعیات فاروق اعظم است ... آنچه از دست فاروق باقی ماند همان است مختلف فیه که تا روز قیامت در آن اتفاق شدنی نیست ۔

for consultation, with a view to taking an agreed decision. It is for this very reason that a case which remained unsettled during their days continued to be a matter of controversy between all the four schools of thought.

The consensus achieved, during the times of the first two caliphs, formed the very basis of these schools. It is, therefore, that a case which is found in them (the schools) having the backing of the unanimous opinion is the same one as had been passed on by the Shaikhain (Abū Bakr and 'Umar). But, how can persons whose knowledge is confined to *Qudūrī*, *Wiqāyah* and *Minhāj* understand this point?[39]

The relation of 'Umar's Jurisprudence with the Jurisprudence of all other Jurisconsults is like that of the text with its commentary. For Muslims, there is abundant good in the codification of his Jurisprudence, as it requires that they should take all the schools of thought as one *Sharī'ah*, and never think in terms of separatism. The mutual differences among them about the injunctions of Law should not in any way shake their faith. They should take the opinions of the largest group (*Sawād-i-A'ẓam*) as quite separate from the rare and the uncommon reports, and must recognise the religious authority as binding upon them, and be aware of the role 'Umar played in the propagation of the religion. Accordingly, for the execution of his mission and in the emulation of his policy they must endeavour hard to achieve the aim

39. Ibid., pp. 134-35.

he was always anxiously in pursuit of.

Common Fiqh. Imām Walīyullāh had tried to lead the Muslim community, divided into various sections, on the main road of *Sharī'ah*, and wanted to bridge up the wide gulf between them. The prescription which he prepared for them and which has already been mentioned was that both the Ḥanafī and Shāfi'ī schools be combined and made one, and then whatever therein be found nearest to the Tradition be adopted; and in this connection the help of *Muwaṭṭa'* be sought, which can serve best the purpose of an impartial arbitrator.

The preparation of the common *Fiqh* to which Shāh Ṣāḥib has pointed out will certainly end the religious differences for ever, bring the Muslims closer together and effect unity among them.

Shāh Ṣāḥib himself has written two commentaries of *Muwaṭṭa'*, namely, *al-Muṣaffā* in Persian and *al-Musawwā* in Arabic, the latter one is of great importance and is very popular among the learned. It gives a clear exposition and makes a thorough investigation of all the religious injunctions and includes the injunctions derived from the text of the Holy Qur'ān, and those which were substantiated by famous Traditions. For every problem, it mentions those of the principles which were strong and reliable from the transmission (*riwāyah*) point of view. In addition to that, it consists of those problems which were unanimously agreed upon by the majority of the Companions and their immediate followers. Besides, it also contains those inferences of Imām Mālik which had been followed and adhered to by the Traditionists. This commentary, undoubtedly, is of immense value and utility, in so far as the presentation of the true picture of religion is concerned.

The importance of *Muwaṭṭa'* can be judged from the fact that once on the occasion of Pilgrimage, the Caliph Manṣūr told Imām Mālik that he had taken a firm decision to send copies of his book to all the Muslim countries with an order that they should follow it and no other book. Thereupon Imām Mālik had replied that this should not be done, because people have heard and received various sayings and differing Traditions, and many a differing report has been conveyed to them. They should, therefore, be left to themselves to go by what they have chosen for themselves.[40]

It will not be out of place here to mention the view of Maulānā 'Ubaidullāh Sindhī in this connection:

"We are of those who were engaged in a battle with our enemy who had occupied our country, and in that battle we were defeated. After defeat, we found out the defect which was the cause of our failure. That defect we noticed everywhere in almost all the Muslim countries; and that defect was this that at present, we cannot act according to our existing Jurisprudence. The reason is quite clear. There is difference in our books, there are conflicts among ourselves and there is no unity among our religious leaders. As such, it has become necessary for us to prepare such kind of Jurisprudence as could accommodate all the various schools of thought, and patch up their differences. In this connection *Musawwā* is the best book for our guidance,

40. *Ḥujjatullāh*, Vol. I, p. 145.

because it combines the Jurisprudence of all the four schools of thought. The proper codification of Jurisprudence is again impossible without consulting the Tradition, and here also *Muwaṭṭa'* of Mālik is sufficient. And if we have an intention to establish an Islamic State in the proper sense of the word, then we will have to prepare and preserve this kind of Jurisprudence; if not, the dream of establishing an Islamic State cannot be realised. Again, if we fail to establish an Islamic State, there remains only the Holy Qur'ān with us, and this is a known fact that the Qur'ān needs explanation at some places, and it is *Muwaṭṭa'* alone which provides such an explanation. The *Muwaṭṭa'* again stands in need of an explanation and for that all the five authentic books, namely, *Bukhārī, Muslim, Tirmidhī, Abū Dāwūd* and *Nasā'ī* are required. Now when it is our duty to teach the Holy Qur'ān to our people, it is but necessary that we should endure for this purpose all the hardships and try to overcome the difficulties. If we ourselves can teach the Qur'ān to them, well and good, otherwise we should at least provide them with needed guidance."[41]

Right Course. In relation to the bye-laws (*Furū'āt*) Shāh Walīyullāh's policy all along had been to follow what both Abū Ḥanīfah and Shāfi'ī had agreed upon. In case of their disagreement he followed that which tallied most with the outward meaning of the Tradition.[42]

Similarly, in the problems of Jurisprudence, his procedure had been to harmonise all the four schools of thought as far as possible, but where harmonisation was found difficult, he used to follow that school which appeared stronger from the point of evidence and the plain Tradition. God had blessed him with the

41. *Risālatun fi Musṭalaḥ-i-Ḥadith wa Sharḥ-i-Ba'ḍ 'Ibārāt in-Nukhbat min Ifādāt 'Ubaidullāh Sindhi.*

42 *Tafhimāt*, Vol. II, p. 202.

abundant wealth of knowledge which enabled him to distinguish the weak from the strong, and answer any question according to any school of thought.[43]

He knew full well how to explain the sayings of the ancients, and was so well aware of their differences and the causes which had given rise to them, that it looked as if he was seeing this all before his eyes.[44]

It is necessary for the Jurists, he says, not to be so motivated by their own principles as to reject the authoritative Tradition and report, and even in the deduction of questions, the proper way is to avoid causing difference and instead one should work for effecting an adjustment. This is the reason why he in his *'Iqd-ul-Jīd*, instead of showing that in the analogical deduction made by the scholars, only one could be right and correct, gave preference to the view that all of them were right and correct and by so doing he had brought to an end all the differences of the bye-laws.

This definitely shows that a follower of one school of thought can avail of the injunction of the other school of thought, if necessary.[45]

It goes to his credit that he never allowed prejudice to come in his way and never gave up the side of truth and justice while making inferences.[46]

He always remained in search of truth. At one place he clearly states that "where the Companions

43. *Ḥayāt-i-Wali*, pp. 496-97.
44. *Tafhimāt*, Vol. I, pp. 148-50.
45. Shāh 'Abd-ul-'Azīz, *Fatāwā*.
46. *Ḥujjatullāh*, "Muqaddimah".

be found differing about a certain question, and the sources of their sayings be also known from the Qur'ān and the *Sunnah*, there the sources alone should be consulted with and brought under consideration, and this alone should be taken as a criterion for determining the weight of one question against the other.''[47]

He, however, was of the view that the *Ijtihād* (independent reasoning) of the *Mujtahid*, even though he be a Companion, is not free from going wrong.[48]

In both the Tradition and Jurisprudence he was a perfect scholar and Maulānā 'Ubaidullāh Sindhī rightly ranks him with Imām Mālik and Imam Abū Ḥanīfah.[49]

47. *Al-Muṣaffā*, Vol. I, p. 27 :

و چون صحابہ مختلف شوند و مآخذ اقوال ایشان از کتاب و سنة ظاهر شود تأمل در آن مآخذ باید کرد . . .

48. *Izālat-ul-Khafā'*, Vol. I, p. 19 :

هر چند اجتهاد هر مجتهدی و لوکان صحابیا احتمال خطا دارد ۔

49. *Ilhām-ur-Raḥmān*, p. 228.

Chapter IV

THE TAṢAWWUF

TAṢAWWUF (Mysticism) deals with the inner aspect of religion. It originally aims at getting that enlightenment which can be attained by means of worship and obedience to God. Its ultimate object is *Iḥsān* (goodness) which is the essence and the kernel of the teachings of religion and which nowadays goes by the name of *Ṭarīqah* and *Ma'rifah*. The Holy Prophet has illustrated it with an example: when a servant of God were to stand for worship and prayer to Him, he should be so much engrossed as to feel that he is seeing God or God is seeing him.[1]

As far as the basic spirit of *Taṣawwuf* is concerned, it is enough to say that it existed during the days of the Holy Prophet; it was, however, in a somewhat different form, and had not adopted the present name.[2]

Apart from the important position that *Taṣawwuf* enjoys in the life of the human being, it has many other benefits; that it strengthens the belief in the life after death, and in the light of the Qur'ānic teachings, the *Imān* without this belief is not acceptable. It is a fact that a Ṣūfī in his spiritual progress experiences such realities which a profound philosopher and a learned man fail to attain even after a very long

1. *Qurrat-u -'Ainain*, p. 42.

2. *Al-Qaul-ul-Jamil.*

period of trial and tribulation.[3]

Shāh Walīyullāh learnt the Ṣūfistic system from his father Shaikh 'Abd-ur-Raḥīm, and devoted himself to the practices of the Naqshbandī school of Ṣūfīs.[4]

He links on good authority the line of his learning the Ṣūfistic discipline and mode of conduct in life with the Holy Prophet, but admits that these customs and systems of *Sulūk* (Ṣūfī's journey) were not in vogue and prescribed in a particular form in those days.[5]

In 1143/1730 when he set out for Pilgrimage, he was blessed there in Medina by Shaikh Abū Ṭāhir, the distinguished Traditionist and the famous divine with his rag, which combined all the qualities inherent in the rags of other Ṣūfīs. He returned from there thoroughly versed in the hidden mysteries of mysticism (*Taṣawwuf*), and well acquainted with the knowledge of exoteric and esoteric sciences of its different schools, their various ways leading towards Divinity, and somehow established connection with each one of them directly or indirectly.[6]

Bai'ah. The proof for the legality of *Bai'ah*, he says, can be traced to certain Traditions. For example, in the days of the Holy Prophet, people used to promise fealty for migration and waging holy war (*Jihād*), and at times for the establishment of the pillars of Islam. On certain occasions, they used to swear an oath of fealty that they would remain firm in the battlefield, would faithfully act according to the

3. *Al-Juz'-ul-Laṭif.*
4. Ibid.
5. *Al-Qaul-ul-Jamil.*
6. *Intibāh fi Salāsil Auliyā' Allāh.*

practice of the Prophet and shun all kinds of innovation. According to one correct report, the Holy Prophet administered an oath of fealty to some Anṣār women on condition that they would not weep over their dead, but to plight loyalty (*bai'at kardan*) is not an incumbent duty, nor one who avoids it is in any way a sinner.[7]

After the end of the reign of the Orthodox Caliphs, this system of *Bai'ah* was given up for the fear lest this oath of allegiance may wrongly pass on for an oath of allegiance to a caliph, and consequently become the cause of the break-up of the community.[8]

The system of rag-robing appeared during the days of Junaid of Baghdad. It is, however, an old practice of the Ṣūfīs to place on their disciples a cap or a turban or to put on them a shirt, a cloak or a scarf by way of accepting them as their pupils. This practice is traced back to the Holy Prophet who once on the occasion of his appointing 'Abd-ur-Raḥmān bin 'Auf as a commander of the Army had wrapped a turban on his head.[9]

Attribution. It is worthy to note here that the Ṣūfīs' linking up their connection with Ḥaḍrat 'Alī is not correct, and cannot be proved by any genuine report. Even the fact as to what special connection Ḥasan of Baṣrah had with 'Alī is still unknown. In spite of that we find that all the Ṣūfīs, both the ancient and modern, are agreed that all the paths of

7. *Al-Qaul-ul-Jamīl.* 8. Ibid.
9. *Intibāh fi Salāsil Auliyā' Allāh.*

Ṭarīqah (the road to Ṣūfī's perfection) go back to 'Alī to terminate there.[10]

Shāh Ṣāḥib says that there ought to be some reason behind such a unanimous agreement of the Ṣūfīs. "In my opinion," he says, "the ecstatic sciences have revealed that the inward attribute of attraction (*Jadhb*) of the Ṣūfīs bears strong resemblance to the inward attribute of 'Alī, as he was the first *majdhūb* (attracted) in the community who opened the door of *Jadhb*. It is due to this reason that they, on account of that attribute, took quick notice of it and became of that temper and taste; and this became the cause of Ṣūfīs' attribution to 'Alī whether that attribution was from Ḥasan's side or from someone else's side makes no difference. Accordingly, when the Ṣūfīs received an ordinary proof of Ḥasan's attachment to 'Alī, it created an extraordinary impression on their minds, which subsequently became the cause of their unanimous belief.[11]

In the days of Shāh Walīyullāh, innovations and bad customs had considerably spoiled the purity of Islam. The preachers presented Islam incorrectly, the Jurists were given over to blind imitation, while the learned and the elite were schismatised. The pseudo-mystics who were already demoralised, taking undue advantage of the simpleness and ignorance of the masses, attributed many a funny and strange thing to themselves. They sold religion for worldly gains,

10. *Hama'āt, Hama'* 11 ; *Qurrat-ul-'Ainain*, pp. 298-302.
11. *Qurrat-ul-'Ainain*, p. 307.

and some of them even turned atheists and free-thinkers.[12]

The possession of Sūfīs' attribute is indeed a great fortune but their practices and performances are of no significance. The Sūfīs who do not possess sufficient knowledge of the Qur'ān and the Tradition are, in reality, the robbers and thieves of religion.[13]

Sharī'ah. Shāh Ṣāḥib differed from his contemporaries, both the Ṣūfīs and the dialecticians in respect of man's purpose in life. The former asserted that the real aim in life was self-annihilation and attainment of permanency. The duties imposed by the *Sharī'ah* were actually meant for the realisation of this aim. As the achievement of it was not possible for everyone, the success of a few would suffice. The latter, on the other hand, were of the view that what had come in the *Sahrī'ah* was, in fact, the real aim of life. He, on the contrary, was of the opinion that in regard to the specific form of man, the *Sharī'ah* alone was the very purpose of his life. In other words, it was the very requirement of his nature. It had not been thrust upon him but had been given to him at his request. Consequently, the commandment of the *Sharī'ah*, which is the requirement of man's specific form, is applicable to all the human beings, and is inclusive of all the human individuals, as humanity penetrates all of them. Individual qualities of a few persons are out of

12 *Al-Budūr-ul-Bāzighah*, p. 82 ; *al-Khair-ul-Kathīr*, p. 105 ; *Tafhīmāt*, Vol. I, p. 208.

13. *Tafhīmāt*, Vol. II, p. 202 ; *Waṣiyyat-Nāmah* :

نسبت هائی صوفیه غنیمت کبری است و رسوم ایشان هیچ نمی ارزد -

consideration here.

As a matter of fact, the people were found dominated by the self-commanding evil (*an-Nafs-ul-Ammārah*), and if they had been left to die in that condition, they could not have escaped the sufferings of the life after death. Thus, in order to avert those sufferings from them, God, the Gracious, out of His sheer kindness, sent through His messengers a remedial measure, namely, the *Sharī'ah.*[14]

Self-annihilation and attainment of everlasting state are desired only as a result of certain peculiarities found in some persons who are born sublime and devoted, and God has given them the necessary guidance, but to live a life of detachment and isolation is not the order of the *Sharī'ah*. The language of the Law-giver makes no reference to such a kind of life whatsoever, directly or indirectly. And even if self-annihilation and complete devotion may have some origin somewhere, going too deep into their preliminaries and taking active part in practices required by them is indeed a wild malady, against which precaution ought to be taken. The books and treatises of the Ṣūfīs are certainly an alchemy, and have the healthiest effect on certain minds, but for the common people they are a killing poison. It must be remembered that the persons who, in the case of religious doctrines, give preference to the path of the philosophers over that of the prophets are worse than

14. *Waṣiyyat-Nāmah* ; *Alṭāf-ul-Quds* (with Urdu translation), pp. 24-25, 89-90.

dogs.[15]

The Law-giver has explained the aim and object of the *Sharī'ah*, the details of which are as follows: The human species is created in a form that combines two opposite faculties, namely, the angelic and the bestial. Man's happiness lies in strengthening the former, while his misery lay in supporting the latter. Accordingly, it is his duty to perform works which may add to the strength of the angelic self and reduce the temper and fury of its rival to an extent that it may yield and obey the angelic one.

Besides, the creation of man is such that his self readily accepts the impressions of his actions done with full deliberation. These very impressions cling to his mind, constitute a part of it, continue with it even after his death and become the cause of his reward and punishment. Contrary is the case of the animals. Whatever they do, the effect produced therefrom does not cling to their minds. It is temporal, hence disappears very soon.

Apart from that man's creation is of the peculiar nature. His heart is capable of receiving inspiration and orders from the Holy Fold (*Ḥaẓīrat-ul-Quds*). If he did good in the world, he will, after his death, by virtue of his good deeds, be found bearing resemblance to the angels and will thus find himself in the ever-abiding bliss. But in case actions done by him

15. *Alṭāf-ul-Quds*, pp. 92-95:

رسائل و کتب صوفیه هر چند به نسبت خواص کیمیائی است عجیب التاثیر اما بنسبت عوام سم قاتل است ۔

were repugnant to the nature of the angels, his life there would surely be too bitter and painful for him and the *Sharī'ah* in this connection has provided the needed guidance.[16]

Instructions. Referring to the miracles (*Karāmāt*) of the Ṣūfīs of his times, Shāh Ṣāḥib says that they, on the most part, are merely tricks and jugglaries. One should not be deceived by them or by their large following, as the common people are generally carried away by custom. No doubt, on certain occasions, some holy persons do perform extraordinary acts out of good motive, but they do not count them as miracles. It is the simpletons who take them to be as such. The remedy to root out this evil lies in reading the books of the Traditions, like those of Bukhārī, Muslim, Abū Dāwūd and Tirmidhī, and by studying the Ḥanafī and Shāfi'ī Jurisprudence, and acting according to the simple practice of the Holy Prophet.[17]

However, in a case where the real love of God happens to take place in the heart of a man and he feels an intense longing for the search of the Ṣūfī path, then at that time he should consult '*Awārif* and side by side read some Naqshbandī treatises, which suggest means of maintaining the "Recollection" (*Yād-dāsht*). In addition to that, he should observe those invocations (to God) which are suggested by the *Sharī'ah*, dress himself with clothes like those of the common people and lead his life according to them.

16. *Ḥujjatullāh*, Vol. I, p. 34.
17. *Waṣiyyat-Nāmah* ; *Maktūbāt* (*Kalimāt-i-Ṭayyibāt*), p. 174.

After reading the books as mentioned, and following the advice given, he will have had no need to look for any spiritual guide for further instructions.[18]

Religious Duty. Among the holy persons, says Shāh Ṣāḥib, there are some who at times are informed through inspiration that they are free from the observance of the duties of the *Sharī'ah* and performance or otherwise of the acts of worship and obedience is left to their choice. He further states that both his father and his uncle were similarly inspired.

On the one hand, he asserts that the inspiration which they received was true, and on the other hand he holds the view that no person can be absolved of the obligation of Law. However, in resolving this difference, he explains it as follows: "In my opinion, the reality of such an inspiration is that, while obeying the injunctions of Law, when a man, progressing by means of his 'faith in the Unseen,' reaches a stage where he happens to acquire faith in them (in the injunctions of Law) through clear proofs, he does not find the obligations of the *Sharī'ah* as anything thrust upon him from outside, but, on the contrary, begins to feel the necessity of those prescribed duties, as one feels that of hunger and thirst, and in that stage he is quite helpless to divest himself of them. Thus, the question of the imposition of duties against the requirement of one's nature does not arise. For such a perfect Ṣūfī, the worship of God is just like his

18. *Waṣiyyat-Nāmah*; *Hama'āt, Hama'*, 7; *Kalimāt-i-Tayyibāt*, p. 174. [*'Awārif-ul-Ma'ārif fi't-Taṣawwuf*, by Suhrawardī (d. 631/1234).]

meeting his natural requirements. The injunctions of Law become an integral part of his nature, as if he was created as such.[19]

Ancient and Modern Ṣūfīs. The ancient Ṣūfīs used to care for the purification of the body, mind and will (*Nafs*, *Qalb* and *'Aql*), gave priority to the disciplining of them, and considered perseverance in the service (*'Ubūdīyyah*) of God as the completion of it (of discipline) ; but the Ṣūfīs who came later did not first engage themselves in anything save the service and in that they were perfectly correct, because if a man succeeds in acquiring the degree of perseverance in the service of God, then it is immaterial for him if something from the Unseen is not disclosed to him. It is, therefore, that Shaikh Bāyazīd of Bisṭām has reckoned that man a king of the praisers of God who practised perseverance in service, but failed in the achievement of any "station" (*Maqām*).

However, the way to improve and reform all the latent faculties is the continuation of the service of God. It, therefore, behoves a man always to apply himself inwardly and outwardly to the service and remembrance of God, so that every limb of his body may have its due share of that service and remembrance.

Maqām *and* Ḥāl. *Maqām* (station) is a quality which a Ṣūfī is expected to attain during his journey towards his Master, so that it (journey) may become complete. The word *Maqām* has a wider definition

19. *Fuyūḍ-ul-Ḥaramain*, Mashhad, p. 7.

which admits of the various "states" (*aḥwāl*), different times and different capabilities. One man finds the "station" in one form, while the other in quite a different shape. *Ḥāl* (state) again is the name of the fruit of the station. In other words, it is the name of its particular form which appears to a particular person according to his particular capability at a particular time. It is, therefore, that *Maqām* is termed the acquired (*Muktasab*) and *Ḥāl* is called the gift of God (*Mauhibah*). For example, the abandonment of desires is a station (*Maqām*) and its fruit, namely, the serene state occasioned by the abandonment which the soul acquires is called the "state" (*Ḥāl*). *Ḥāl*, however, is temporal and timely, and cannot last for ever. The story of Hanẓalah al-Asīdī is an apt illustration of that.

One day when Abū Bakr asked him about his condition, he replied : "I have become a hypocrite, because when we hear of Paradise and Hell from the Holy Prophet, it appears as if we are actually seeing them with our eyes, but no sooner we return home than we forget much of it due to our other engagements." Thereupon Abū Bakr said, "In reality, same is the case with me." Accordingly, they both went to the Prophet and apprised him of their condition, who replied, "If you continue to be in the same condition, then the angels will be found from every side shaking hands with you. But remember, Ḥanẓalah, this condition takes place sparingly."[20]

20. *Ḥujjatullāh*, Vol. II, pp. 94-95.

Whatever difference is apparently seen in the "states" and the "stations" of the holy persons is the result of the difference in their capabilities (*Isti'dādāt*). They appear to them according to their individual aptitudes. It has come in the Tradition that if you hear the mountain having shifted away from its place, you may believe, but if you hear of a man having changed his nature, believe it not, because every man returns to his original nature. In this Tradition, the word *khalq* (nature) means capability.[21]

Laṭā'if. Herein below is the account of man's *Laṭā'if*, namely, the body, the mind and the will (*Nafs, Qalb* and *'Aql*).

In the body of man there are three vital members by means of which all the acts and purposes which man's specific form requires are served. For example, the seat of perceptive faculties is the brain, the seat of anger, rashness, grief and joy is the heart, while the seat of things without which body cannot survive, like eating, drinking and sleeping, etc., is the liver. The Sūfīs, however, assert that these vital members have internal powers, in addition to the external ones, and they call them by the name of *Laṭā'if*. On that account, these three members are well known by the names of *Laṭīfat-ul-'Aql, Laṭīfat-ul-Qalb* and *Laṭīfat-un-Nafs*.[22]

21. *Hama'āt, Hama'* 18:
بدانکه اکثر اختلاف احوال اهل الله بر اختلاف استعدادات ایشان مبتنی است ۔

22. *Ḥujjatullāh*, Vol. II. p. 90.

Shāh Walīyullāh is of the opinion that, in addition to these three *Laṭā'if*, there is a fourth one also, which he names as *Laītfat-ul-Jawāriḥ*. According to him, all the injunctions of the Law (*Sharī'ah*) have their connection with this *Laṭīfah* and, from the side of the Law, man will be required to account for only those of his actions which resulted from this *Laṭīfah*. A brief description of it is as follows: When all the powers of *Qalb*, *'Aql* and *Nafs* become a pivot for the complete functioning of the limbs of the body, or, in other words, when all the activities of the *Qalb*, *'Aql* and *Nafs* are absorbed into the working of the limbs of the body, then that state gained is called *Laṭīfat-ul-Jawāriḥ*. For the explanation of this *Laṭīfah* he says: "Once a camel was shown to me which was on the point of dying. All its three *Laṭā'if* had gone very weak, and it was reined with a file of camels; there was no energy left in it save the movement. It, however, continued moving till it fell down and died. At this kind of its death, I was told that it was absorbed in the *Laṭīfat-ul-Jawāriḥ*." From the *Sharī'ah's* side, man would be made to give an account of his actions which emanated from this *Laṭīfah* only, and the *Sharī'ah* is solely concerned with this *Laṭīfah*.[23]

Investigation, says Shāh Ṣāḥib, has shown that every limb of the body and each one of these *Laṭā'if* has its own duty to perform, and its own business to look after; but when they unite, their union gives rise to twofold state. Either they so mix up with each

23. *Alṭāf-ul-Quds*, p. 30.

other and get united as are water and silver mixed up and united in mercury, or each one of them remains independent in its own place and helps the other when necessary, in the build-up of the body. From the first state accrue the prevalence (*Ghalàbah*), the self-effacement, the absorption (*Maḥw*) in the Deity and the ecstasy (*Wajd*), while from the second are gained the sobriety (*Saḥw*), the establishment (*Ṭamkīn*) and the constancy (*Istiqlāl*). The ripe Ṣūfī is, however, he who maintains unmixed establishment and whose every *Laṭīfah* is independent in itself.[24]

One form of the prevalence is that of the desire which is born after the light of the faith had penetrated into the heart, even though it had been for or against the Law (*Sharī'ah*). Law in its injunctions, however, embraced a variety of purposes which are beyond the comprehension of a believer; he, therefore, at times is tended towards mercy where it should not have been shown. The other form of the prevalence is the result of the inebriation (*Sukr*). Here, the light of faith so overpowers both the reason and the heart that he gives up all the charms of life, and begins to like things which are often disliked. For an example, Abū Dardā'ī used to say: "On account of my desire to meet my Lord, I eagerly wish for death, and consider sickness better as it is an expiation of sins."

An example of the self-effacement is that when once 'Abdullāh b. 'Umar was busy in the circumam-

24. Ibid., p. 66

bulation of the Ka'bah and a man saluted him, he had not returned the salutation. Later on, when his attention was drawn towards it he replied, "At that time we were seeing God; therefore, forgot all else."[25]

We have mentioned it repeatedly that the resolution of differences is an outstanding merit of Shāh Walīyullāh. Here below a couple of such examples are given:

(1) Jesus Christ says that the other-worldly blisses will be spiritual, while the Holy Prophet Muhammad has said that they would be material.

Imām Walīyullāh brings an agreement between the two through the *Tajallī-i-A'ẓam*, the Great Emanation (*al-Wujūd-ul-Munbasiṭ*: Unfolding Existence). He explains that the *Tajallī-i-A'ẓam* which is the fountainhead of all the powers in existence is capable of assuming different forms, as it has come in the Qur'ān: "Every day in (new) splendour (state) does He (shine)."[26] The Prophets who are the interpreters of the Unseen World can give news of only that form of the splendour which appeared in their age, and for which they were raised. They, however, through their intuition, can perceive the things of the Hereafter, and comprehend many other hidden sciences. But the *Laṭīfah* which dominates their nature quickly asserts itself, with the result that their news given is according to its (*Laṭīfah's*) requirements. The "state" or "splendour" of which Jesus was the interpreter

25. *Ḥujjatullāh*, Vol. II, pp. 90-94.
26. Sūrah ar-Raḥmān, Verse 29.

was inclined to the hidden faculties of man, like *Ḥijr Baḥt, Laṭīfat-us-Sirr* and *Laṭīfat-ur-Rūḥ*, and the *Tajallī-i-A'ẓam* made its appearance in those faculties (*Laṭā'if*). The "state" or the "splendour" the spokesman of which was the Prophet Muḥammad had its inclination towards the manifest faculties of man like *Laṭīfat-ul-Qalb, Laṭīfat-un-Nafs, Laṭīfat-ul-'Aql* and *Laṭīfat-ul-Jawāriḥ*. Thus, the *Tajallī-i-A'ẓam* manifested itself in them. This actually was the cause of some difference in the Laws (*Sharā'i'*) of the Prophets, as well as in their information given about the affairs of the Hereafter.[27]

(2) Waḥdat-ul-Wujūd. The doctrine of the "Unity of Being" (*Waḥdat-ul-Wujūd*) and that of the Unity of Appearance (*Waḥdat-ush-Shuhūd*) were keenly discussed during the days of Shāh Walīyullāh. Shaikh Muḥy-ud-Dīn Ibn-ul-'Arabī has affirmed the doctrine of *Waḥdat-ul-Wujūd* and Shāh Ṣāḥib also held that belief, but about a hundred years before him, Imām Rabbānī introduced anew the doctrine of *Waḥdat-ush-Shuhūd*. His contention was that it is in fact the "Unity of Appearance" which a Ṣūfī takes to be the Unity of Being (*Waḥdat-ul-Wujūd*). In other words, what he in his spiritual progress sees at that station is, in reality, the shadow of the original truth (God), which is far, far away from him.[28]

27. *Tafhīmāt*, Vol. I, pp. 116, 127 ; *Fuyūḍ-ul-Ḥaramain*, Mashhad, p. 11. *Ḥijr Baḥt* (Pure Intellect), a technical term employed by Shāh Ṣāḥib, signifies the presence of a specimen of the *Tajjalli-i-A'ẓam* in the heart of man (*Saṭa'āt, Saṭa'* 18).

28. Imām Rabbānī, *Maktūbāt*, VI, I, *Maktūb* 260.

Some people, says Shāh Ṣāḥib, have presented the words of Shaikh Ibn-ul-'Arabī with comments in a way that created an impression of his belief in the doctrine of the real Unity of Being, but this is absolutely wrong. He, however, believed only in the "Shadowy Unity of God". Having examined the works of both, he has clearly shown that there is no reasonable difference between their views. The difference in phraseology carries no meaning, and the purpose of both is exactly the same. The *Waḥdat-ush-Shuhūd* of Imām Rabbānī is in no way different from the *Waḥdat-ul-Wujūd* of Ibn-ul-'Arabī, which he explains as follows:

"Zaid, 'Umar and Bakr, etc., are essentially the same from the point of human nature (humanity) which is common among all. The species of man and the species of animal are also the same in the sense that animality (animal life and nature) is commonly shared by both. Similarly, this whole universe has also a self (*nafs*) as an individual person has a self, which is called the Universal Soul (*an-Nafs-ul-Kullīyah*). The multiplicity of the whole universe has originated from it. Now when Ibn-ul-'Arabī says that everything is God, he thereby means the Universal Soul. This Universal Soul, or the Self-unfolding Being (*al-Wujūd-ul-Munbasiṭ*), subsists by itself and is the cause of the subsistence of everything other than itself. This existence pervades the whole universe, both the substance and the accident, and accepts the form of everything. It is both immanent and transcendental. Beyond this existence (*al-Wujūd-ul-Munbasiṭ*: Universal Soul) towards the original existence (God) none has an access to. In other words, man's progress ends with the Universal Soul or the Self-unfolding Being. He cannot move a step further. The Universal Soul and God are so intermingled that the former is often taken for the latter."

Now remains the question of the relation that

this existence (*al-Wujūd-ul-Munbasiṭ*) has with the essence of God itself. This relation is, however, known only in its reality (*annīyyah* : I-ness) ; its quality is unknown and can never be known.[29] Thus, when Ibn-ul-'Arabī says that the realities of the existing things are the names and the attributes of the Universal Soul (Self-unfolding Being) in the stage of knowledge (*Fī Martabat-il-'Ilm*, in the Divine Consciousness) or when Imām Rabbānī asserts that the realities of existing objects are sheer nothingnesses on which the lights of the names and attributes of the Universal Soul (*al-Wujūd-ul-Munbasiṭ*) are reflected is exactly the same thing. The difference in their language is so little that it needs no consideration.[30]

This point, however, can be fairly understood by a parable. Let our universe be taken as a mirror for the sun of Reality. When we see the reflection of the sun in the mirror, we take it to be the sun itself—and this is the idea of the "Real Unity of Being"—but at times we say that the sun which is seen in the mirror is only the reflection of the original one, which is far, far away. This is what is meant by the "Shadowy Appearance of Being".

By giving such an explanation of the doctrine of *Waḥdat-ul-Wujūd* and *Waḥdat-ush-Shuhūd*, Shāh Ṣāḥib has indeed reconciled the viewpoints of both the Semites and the Aryans. The Semitic mind believes God to be immune and immaterial, transcending the

29. *Alṭāf-ul-Quds*, p. 105 :

نسبتی است معلوم الانیة مجهول الکیفیة -

30. *Maktūb-i-Madani* ; *Lamaḥāt*, *Lamḥah* 21.

objects of Nature, while the Aryan mind sees Him in the manifestation of existence and believes Him making His appearance in the phenomenon of Nature. The one believes in the transcendence of God and the other in His immanence. God's connection with the universe is approximately the same the soul has with the body.

Four Periods of Mysticism. There are four periods in the history of mysticism. The first one is of the first and the second century of Islam, in which the outcome of mysticism and the sumtotal of religion was *Iḥsān.* The second one begins with Junaid of Baghdad. In that period the stress was laid on the acquisition of the attributes of "Attachment with God" (*Ta'alluq-billāh*). The third period starts with Shaikh Abū Sa'īd b. Abi'l-Khair and Shaikh Abu'l-Ḥasan of Khirqān, in which the mystics crossing the bar of actions acquired the degree of *Jadhb* (Attraction). The last one is that of Ibn-ul-'Arabī, in which other relevant problems of mysticism were discussed; for example, the emanation of this universe from the Self-Existent (*Wājib-ul-Wujūd*). Shāh Ṣāḥib, however, claims to have combined in his person all the attributes of the mystics of these four periods.[31]

He opines that all these different periods which followed in the history of mysticism were to the liking of God. As such, whenever a case of a certain Ṣūfī be discussed, it is necessary to look into the state of his *Laṭīfah* in the light of the prevailing conditions.

31. *Hama'āt, Hama's* 1, 2, 16.

The present age demands that whatever knowledge we have, whether rational, traditional or mystical, we should try as far as possible to effect agreement and remove discrepancies wherever they be. Let every saying or utterance be placed in its proper place and treated accordingly.[32]

During his lifetime, Greek philosophy had widely spread and influenced the young minds considerably. In reference to that, he calls upon people to turn to the Qur'ān and the Tradition, as they are the real sources of knowledge. He severely criticised those Ṣūfīs who put up an artificial show. His appeal to the learned, the theologians and the Ṣūfīs was to work zealously for the preaching and propagation of Islam and public demonstration of its practices and see Islam gaining force everywhere. The absence of such activities, he laments, is indicative of the absence of such zealous workers and missionaries who aim at the prevalence of Islam.[33]

In his *al-Qaul-ul-Jamīl*, his exhortations are as follows:

"Keep yourself away from the society of the wealthy and the chiefs, who are generally inclined to the imitation of foreign fashions. You can visit them sparingly only for some good work and for the repelling of an injustice. Have no connection whatsoever with an ignorant Ṣūfī who deceitfully keeps himself away from the observance of the religious duties, and also refrain from the company of that foolish, worshipping devotee who practises undue austerity without justification. You should further shun the society of those theologians who show extreme

32. *Maktūb-i-Madani*.
33. *Tafhimāt*, Vol. I, pp. 82, 215.

indifference towards the things of this world and are happy at the utterances of the dead and have neglected the clear injunctions of the Holy Prophet. You should always follow the course of moderation. In addition, you should guard yourself against falling into the trap of the contentious *Ma'qūlī* (rationalist) who is prone to create doubts."[34]

Shāh Ṣāḥib was not only a man of learning, but also a person of vision and "taste" (*dhauq*). He never accepted anything until its truth was confirmed by both, the tradition and the reason. The fact is that when the principles of mysticism were systematically arranged and brought into writing they after a long passage of time, on account of the difference in the capabilities (*Isti'dādāt*) of the mystics, got mixed up with the principles of prophecy, thus making it difficult to draw a dividing line between the two. He clearly separated one from the other and placed every expression and saying in its proper place and removed the confusion wherever it was.[35]

34. *Ḥayāt-i-Wali*, pp. 531-32.
35. *Nuzhat-ul-Khawāṭir*, Vol, VI, p. 402.

Chapter V

THE PROPHECY

PROPHECY (*Nubuwwah*) is not something which could be acquired through bodily and spiritual gymnastics, nor is it inborn in the sense that the self of the prophet has been created in such a way that he is compelled to perform actions corresponding to purity. The prophecy, on the other hand, is the highest degree conferred at an appointed time.[1]

Advent of the Prophet. When the condition of the world worsens and there is chaos everywhere, God raises a prophet to assist in the rescue of the suffering humanity, and to restore peace and order. Whoever at that time is found as the holiest, most veracious and determined among the people is inspired to rise and command people to practise virtue and shun vice. Then those who obey and answer his call are saved and favoured. He is also ordered to wage war against those who oppose and resist, both with the sword and with the tongue, and continue his fight, until the vicious and the vile are separted from the virtuous.

The person chosen on the occasion, namely, the prophet, then becomes an object of Divine Support and Blessing, and receives a revelation which fills his heart

1. *Izālat-ul-Khafā'*, Vol. I, p. 51 :

پیش اهل حق نبوت مکتسب نیست - - - و نه امری است جبلی - - - -

with both exoteric and esoteric knowledge. Accordingly, he becomes well aware and cognizant of the Divine Will, which, descending from the highest heavens, comes upon his heart, dressed in the clothes of words and letters. That occasion is the exact time about which, in the terminology of the *Sharī'ah*, it is said that such a one has been sent by God as a prophet, and has been ordered to preach and convey His message. This degree of prophecy is, however, awarded to one whose self is pure, who by his birth is counted among the "Sublime Assembly" (*al-Mala'-ul-A'lā*) and whose angelic powers are unusually bright and dominating. He is perfect in health, and is free from the physical weaknesses.[2]

Qualities. The nature (*ṭabī'ah*) of such a prophet, in spite of being too strong, is submissive to his heart, his heart, despite being very vigorous and firm, always obeys his reason, his reason again, though extraordinarily clear and sound, bows to the "Sublime Assembly" (*al-Mala'-ul-A'lā*), and he is, in a way, a true copy of it. As his intellectual faculty bears complete resemblance to it (*al-Mala'-ul-A'lā*), he readily accepts the revelation, and then the real knowledge, particularly that which relates to the species of man and other excellent morals, automatically gushes out from the recesses of his heart without any effort or learning. His practical power is of utmost rectitude; as such, infallibility happens to be one of his qualities. By virtue

2. Ibid. (*al-Mala'-ul-A'lā*, a hierarchy in Heaven under God's command, discusses questions of high import in the universe).

of his greatest possible resemblance with the "Universal Soul" (*al-Nafs-ul-Kullīyah*), he becomes a tool in its hand for the manifestation of laws and sciences concerning humanity and serves as a shining lamp for its guidance in matters both worldly and other-worldly.

When he is sent from God and an aspect imitating the Great Man (*Insān Kabīr*) is reflected on the tablet of his heart, then all the human individuals are joined to his knowledge and his perfection like one connected chain. He then chooses a plan by which he considers the forms of all the people near and afar, young and old, male and female, as if he sees them all from afar.[3] Regarding this much about prophecy, no one has any doubt. All the people are agreed, not only on its possibility, but on its coming into existence as well. This is the reason why we find every community reverently following its saintly persons, as it finds in them the extraordinary power of imagination and of quick understanding. The only difference among it (community) is whether an angel came to him (prophet), and God spoke to him or not.[4]

The heart of this perfect man (the prophet) represents sciences in which lie the success and prosperity of the people. This representation sometimes appears to him in the form of a dream, and at times in the form of a revelation, and on certain occasions in the shape of an angel, who speaks to him face to

3. *Al-Budūr-ul-Bāzighah*, p. 196.
4. Ibid., pp. 168-69 ; *Izālat-ul-Khafā'*, Vol. II, p. 52.

face and conveys to him the message of God. He (God) always lends support to his friends and followers, and helps them prevail over their enemies. This is, in reality, the origin of prophecy. God's blessings are being continuously showered upon him with the result that on some occasions certain things happen which customarily do not happen, and these go by the name of miracles.[5]

Definition of Prophecy. The Ash'arī school of thought gives the definition of prophecy as follow: "Prophet is he about whom God said that He has raised him as a prophet, who has conveyed His message to the people and to whom God has spoken some such words. There is no condition set for being a prophet. Whomsoever He likes, He makes him a prophet." This definition is such that to call oneself a prophet can be the business of the prophet only, because people in general will not otherwise come to know whether God ever spoke to him. Speaking on the reality of prophecy, Imām Rāzī remarks that prophecy is the name of the perfection of intellectual and practical faculties, and miracles have nothing to do with it. Imām Ghazālī is of view that if a man wants to know the truth about a prophet, then he should think over his words and deeds, the guidance and the direction he has given, and not to his having transformed a rod into a serpent or cloven up the moon.[6]

5. *Ḥujjatullāh*, Vol. I, p 16 : *Ta'wil-ul-Aḥādith*, pp. 60-61.

6. *Al-Munqidh Min aḍ-Ḍalāl* :

فمن ذالک الطریق فالطلب الیقین بالنبوة لا من قلب العصا ثعبانا وشق القمر ۔

Different Forms of Prophecy. Shāh Walīyullāh further states that the form of prophecy changes with the change of time. The prophet sometimes appears in the form of a king and a caliph, at times in the garb of a profound scholar, and on certain other occasions in the shape of a hermit and a spiritual guide. Similarly, there are different causes for the advent of the prophets, and their works and their performances have also varied. Before the Prophet Noah, the prophets appeared in the form of a thinker and a philosopher.[7]

The Prophet Muḥammad combined in himself the requisite qualities of a ruler, a caliph, a profound scholar, a hermit and a spiritual guide.[8]

There are, however, certain attributes which have no connection with the origin and essence of prophecy, such as the fascinating beauty, superior lineage, sweet voice, eloquence, wealth and bodily power.[9]

Infallibility of Prophet. One of the attributes necessarily to be found in a prophet is that he should be strong both intellectually and practically to an extent that he may look prominent and distinguished from the rest of the people. All his knowledge and

7. *Tafhimāt*, Vol. I, p. 75 :

پیش از نوح نبوت شبیه بحکمة و رویة بود -

8. *Izālat-ul-Khafā'*, Vol. I, p. 259 ; Vol. II, p. 1.

9. *Qurrat-ul-'Ainain*, pp. 39, 178, 195 : *Tafhimāt*, Vol. I, p. 178 :

حضرت پیغامبر ما صلعم کمال همه جمع فرموده بود که بعض ان باصل نبوت لازم نیست مثال جمال رائع ، و نسب بارع و صوت حسن و قوت بطش - - - کثرة المال و صباحة الوجه - - - و فصاحت لسان باعتبار ذات خود با خلافت نبوت ربطی ندارد -

sciences should be a God-given gift, and not the outcome of any thinking or reflection as happens in the case of the common man. He should be an embodiment of sinlessness, and do nothing against the Law (*Sharī'ah*). Sinless, of course, he ought to be, because the impression of what God likes and dislikes appears in the Holy Fold (*Ḥaẓīrat-ul-Quds*) and he, being its reflexive mirror, becomes at once aware of it. As such, the question of his sinning does not arise.

Divine Protection. Besides, God protects the prophets from their falling into any kind of error in three ways:

(1) He creates them with a sound nature (*fiṭrah*), free from weakness.

(2) He informs them by means of an inspiration about the consequences of the good and bad actions.

(3) At times, He puts obstructions between them and the evil actions through the show of Unseen powers, as it happened in the case of the Prophet Yūsuf (Joseph) when he was being seduced by the wife of 'Azīz. His father Ya'qūb (Jacob) had appeared to him on that occasion while he (Ya'qūb) was biting his finger.[10]

In addition to these attributes, God wishes his prevalence, his success, the raising of his prestige, and the elevation of his rank. He and his followers are always made victorious and graced and their enemies vanquished and disgraced. He may, at times,

10. *Ḥusn-ul-'Aqīdah*.

see in his dreams the coming events, which afterwards occur and come out to be true. His mind may be so broad, expanded and replete with noble sciences and high ambitions, that he should be fit enough to fulfil the Divine Will.

Apart from that, his obedience is made obligatory on the people, and his religion and his prevalence are to last for a very long time. He performs miracles and, at times, knows even the secrets of hearts and his prayers are generally accepted. On certain occasions, he makes demonstration of his extraordinary power and his exorcism proves efficacious. He is completely self-disciplined and possesses an amazing power of discernment. In short, the prophet combines the qualities of the following five persons :

(1) A king and a ruler, a social reformer and a warner who effects unity and order among people and has the knowledge of the trials, the evils of devil and the knowledge of the Resurrection and its portents.

(2) A philosopher, with an abundant share of practical knowledge, well acquainted both in reality and in practice with the ethical philosophy, household economy and state administration.

(3) A mystic guide, who sits in the circle of mystics and works wonders, and who with the force of his guidance brings the deviating to the road of salvation, and who knows well how the diseased minds are cured through

acts of obedience and self-mortification.

(4) A witness, who may be knowing the ranks of the people and the degrees according to their perfection, and may be knowing the actions and their reward both in this world and in the Hereafter. He may also have the knowledge of the events which are to take place in the stage of the grave, on the Day of Gathering, and of what is in Paradise and in Hell.

(5) Gabriel, who is an instrument in the hand of God for serving His purpose, always ready to carry His command and put it into action.[11]

Great Prophet. The great and the best prophet is he who holds the office of the prophet and that of the vicegerent, one whose advent implies the twofold object: to bring people out of darkness into light, and to see that his community turns out to be good and a useful guide for the other communities. The advent of the Holy Prophet Muḥammad was of this nature. In reference to the first, the words of the Qur'ān are: "He Who sent among the illiterate a messenger from among them," and in reference to the second, it says: "You are the best community raised for mankind." Thus, the superior prophet is he who surpasses others in doing the greatest good to mankind and from whom the world receives the maximum of beneficence.[12]

11. *Qurrat-ul-'Ainain*, pp. 40-43; *Izālat-ul-Khafā'*, Vol. I, p. 259; Vol. II, p. 1; *al-Budūr-ul-Bāzighah*, p. 174.

12. *Ḥujjatullāh*, Vol. I, p. 84. Sūrah al-Jumu'ah, verse 2; Sūrah Āl-i-'Imrān, verse 109.

If one is to judge the superiority of the Holy Prophet in terms of his good actions, then the followers of other prophets can prove such actions in their own prophets as well. If the community of a prophet happens to be numerically large and if his advent has proved more beneficial to mankind than that of the other prophets, then his superiority is confirmed.

In this connection, Shāh Ṣāhib quotes the Tradition of the Holy Prophet: "I will vie with the other communities through you in number," and explains that it hints at his superiority due to the large number of his community rather than the purity of his intention. The greater the number of the community, the greater would be the flow of Divine Bounty. His being the mercy for all the worlds and for all the times to come is a solid proof and a clear indication of his being the best.[13]

Despite being the best of mankind, he is reported to have said that he should not be taken as superior to Prophet Yūnus (Jonah). It is so because, giving preference to one over the other, invariably, becomes the cause of the other's under-estimation.

It should be borne in mind, says Shāh Walīyullāh at some other place, that the superiority of the prophets is mainly based on the capabilities of their fixed prototypes (*a'yān thābitah*) which are, however,

13. *Tafhimāt*, Vol. I, pp. 243-44 ; *Izālat-ul-Khafā'*, p. 314 :
آنحضرت صلعم باعتبار صحت نیت افضل نشدند از آن انبیاء که امت ایشان کم بود از امت آنحضرت صلعم ، بلکه هر چند امت بیشتر جارحیت فیوض الاهی قوی تر -

different. Every prophet was given a certain Law which was absolutely sound. The difference in their Laws is the result of the different ways they received them from their Lord on account of their differing fixed prototypes. Thus, the question of their superiority in respect of the soundness of Laws does not arise. Their superiority is entirely dependent upon their eternal perfections and runs in proportion to the capabilities of their fixed prototypes.[14]

This is a fact that no rank of any of the prophets has so much surprised the Peripatetic philosophers and others as the rank of the two great prophets, Moses and Muḥammad, the reason being that they had devoted themselves to the achievement of the required qualities with their collective brain-faculties, till they became separate from the rest of the people in every respect.[15]

It is worthy to note here that the prophets are generally revolutionaries; and if a prophet has to achieve prevalence, then the way towards it is not that there should be an angel with him certifying his being a prophet or that a book should descend upon him from heaven and the people see it descending with their eyes, but just as the worldly kings prevail upon their opponents through struggle and the use of force, similarly the prophets also achieve their

14. *Al-Khair-ul-Kathir*, p. 73:

وليس هناك فضل الا فى الكمالات الازلية - - - وانما التفاضل بحسب استعداد الاعيان -

15. *Al-Budūr-ul-Bāzighah*, p 175.

purpose through fighting and waging of wars. This is a fact which Shāh Ṣāḥib asserts has been testified by his intuition.[16]

Prophecy below Nature. Some mention has already been made of the causes which necessitate the advent of a prophet. Their true knowledge is of course with God only, but there are certain causes which when found make the advent of the prophet unavoidable. The great events like the raising of a prophet generally take place sparingly, when both the earthly and the heavenly causes combine together to press for that. However, when the prophet comes, it is always the relative good which is kept in view. In other words, when the emergence of the relative good is dependent upon the advent of the prophet, he is raised by God. Again, when the prophet comes, he does not enjoin upon people what their nature is opposed to, because prophecy is always below nature. The prophet's job is to improve and perfect things as they ought to be improved and perfected, and cleanse the hearts of people in such a way that they may have good faith in God and begin to perform actions which may bring their salvation here and in the Hereafter. Besides, his duty is to teach them a true lesson of sincerity (*Ikhlāṣ*) and of beneficence

16. *Fuyūḍ-ul-Ḥaramain*, Mashhad, p. 4 :
ما كانت صورة غلبة الرسول ان يكون معه الملك يشهد له - - - بل كانت صورة غلبة الملوك بالمجاهدات و الحروب ، و هذه قضية قضى بها الوجدان -

(*Iḥsān*), as these are the very essence of religion.[17]

Miracles. It is worthwhile to make here a reference to the miracles of the prophets. One of the signs by which a prophet is distinguished from other people is his working of the miracles. Imām Rāzī, while commenting upon the verse: "Yet they say: why are not signs sent down to him from his Lord?" says that the miracle is not a condition for prophecy. It is for this reason that the prophets like Shīth (son of Adam), Idrīs and Shu'aib are reported to have wrought no miracles. However, people who believe in miracles look upon this act as a symbol of prophecy. Obviously a symbol can never be a reality in itself.[18]

Shāh Walīyullāh excludes the working of miracles from the nature of prophecy, and says that the appearance of miracles is a customary occurrence and is subject to the external causes, but because their causes occur very rarely they also appear very rarely. Many wonderful things are happening in life, but because people are familiar with them, they do not take them as wonderful; and whenever a certain thing with which they are not familiar takes place, they take it to be extraordinary. There were events about which the prophets had given information in advance, and when they actually happened, they were taken as their miracles, as, for example, the

17. *Ḥujjatullāh*. Vol. I. pp. 84-85; *Tafhīmāt*, Vol. I, pp. 68-69:
اعلم ان النبوة من تحت الفطرة -

18. Shiblī, *al-Kalām*, pp. 78-109.

news of the punishment conveyed by the Prophets Hūd and Ṣāliḥ to the people of 'Ād and Thamūd. Nevertheless, it is a fact that, with the majority of the prophets, the miracles go hand in hand, but to subject prophecy to the working of miracles is absolutely incorrect. Whenever a man is put in charge of the office of the prophet, he comes under the constant flow of the Divine Blessings resulting in the form of miracles at his hands. Some wonderful happenings which people generally take to be extraordinary follow their usual course and occur ordinarily.[19]

As long as this world continues, these miraculous happenings will also continue to happen. There are, however, some unusual things which do not separate from the holy man (*walī*). One of them is the subsistence by the Unseen (*Nafqat-ul-Ghaib*), and this holy man receives his subsistence from one or the other place without any effort on his part.

The difference between the talisman, necromancy and phylactery which have been the practice of those who do not follow the course of the prophets, and of those invocations and Divine Names which have been suggested by the prophets is that the intention of the former is to influence the powers of Nature while the object of the latter by their suggested

19. *Ḥujjatullāh*, Vol. I, pp. 16, 85 ; *Hama'āt. Hama'* 21 ; *Ta'wil-ul-Ahādith*, p. 80 ; *Tafhimāt*, Vol. I, p. 100 :

فليست المعجزات ولا استجابة الدعوات و نحو ذالک الا امورا خارجة عن اصل النبوة لازمة فی الاکثر - - - اقول خرق العادة عادة مستمرة - - - الخوارق من الاحوال العادية لما کان اسبابها قليلة الوقوع لا يظهر الا قليلا -

prayers is to win the favour of the Sublime Assembly (*al-Mala'-ul-A'lā*). The man who observes these invocations and Divine Names comes under the mercy of the Holy Fold (*Ḥaẓīrat-ul-Quds*). Consequently the favours of the Sublime Assembly and the mercy of the Holy Fold, then, unitedly come to his help and do the needful.[20]

Ascension. The learned (*ḥukamā'*) are of view that the Ascension (*Mi'rāj*) had taken place in a state of wakefulness, with body which was the perfection incarnate, and not with this body which is composed of elements. When all the singular perfections unite to become one, it (unity) acquires some sort of nearness to God. It is, therefore, necessary that, in all the degrees of spiritual ascendancy, it should have a certain real form. It has come in the Tradition also that the Antichrist (Dajjāl) will appear as an embodiment of evil. But this Ascension took place in a state which was neither material nor spiritual, but just the middle of them, which combined the attributes of both. Spiritual attributes dominated the body and the spiritual ideas (*Ma'ānī*) assumed the bodily form. Splitting of the breast and then filling the heart with faith (*Īmān*) refers to the prevalence of the angelic lights upon the human nature (*Ṭabī'ah*) with the result that its fury subsided and it willingly bowed down to what descended on it from the Holy Fold (*Ḥaẓīrat-ul-Quds*). The Prophet's riding on the "Burāq" refers to his rational soul (*Nafs Nāṭiqah*) which ruled his *Nasmah* (Animal Spirit). In other words, the

20. *Hama'āt, Hama'* 22 ; *Hawāmi'*.

attributes of the rational soul dominated those of the animal self. His journey from one heaven to another heaven is indicative of his spiritual progress stage by stage towards the court of God. By *Sidrat-ul-Muntahā* (the lote tree) is meant the tree of existence (*Kaun*). It has been likened to the tree as the working system of both (tree and existence) is more or less the same.[21]

Revelation and Inspiration. The points differentiating one from the other are many, but some of them are as follows.

(1) In the case of revelation, man's perceptive faculties are first subjugated by the faculties of the "Sublime Assembly" (*al-Mala'-ul-A'lā*), and then starts the flow of knowledge towards him from the "Holy Fold" (*Ḥaẓīrat-ul-Quds*), but in the case of an inspiration, both these things do not happen simultaneously.

(2) If the Divine Grace dominates the capability of the recipient, then it is called a revelation, which is made only to the prophets, and it aims at the reformation of the people. If reverse be the case, then it is the inspiration which comes to the holy persons (*Auliyā'*).

(3) Revelation is always free from any ambiguity, and is extremely clear in its import and purpose. It is so because the intention of God is the good of the world and His intention admits of no

21. *Al-Khair-ul-Kathir*, p. 81 ; *Ḥujjatullāh-ul-Bālighah*, Vol. II, pp. 206-07 :

المعراج و هو عند حزب الحكمة فى اليقظة ببدن من تجسد الكمالات لا من تجوهر العناصر -

change whatsoever. Thus, the revelation of the prophets is a certain science, whether they received it through discernment (*Firāsah*), dream or any inspiration. In the case of *Auliyā'* (holy persons) there is, however, a possibility of some doubt.[22]

(4) Revelation, unlike inspiration, is in no way the creation of the mind and the prophet alone can acquire a state of complete disappearance and his knowledge is of universal penetration.[23]

Again, the Universal Administration (*Tadbīr-i-Kullī*), which is always engaged in looking after the maintenance of the principle of the "survival of the fittest" on the earth, gets pictured in the pure intellect of the prophet, exactly in the same manner as the reflection of the sun gets pictured in the well-polished mirror, with the result that his mental and intellectual faculties begin to shine with its (pure intellect's) light. Thus, when the origin of his sciences is the pure intellect, they are certain and above equivocation, excluding the possibility of any change or doubt.[24]

Revelation of the Qur'ān. Sometimes, God intends that His guidance should continue among people for ever, and that they should hold fast to it and seek His nearness. Consequently, the Divine Grace, subjugating the person of the prophet, summarily inscribes the

22. *Saṭa'āt, Saṭa'* 16, 18 ; *Ta'wil-ul-Aḥādith*, p. 78.
23. *Al-Khair-ul-Kathir*, pp. 34-35.
24. *Saṭa'āt, Saṭ'* 18 :

تدبیر الاهی که مبنی آن اختیار اصلح فالاصلح است فردی کاملی را جارحه سازند - - -

Book of God in his pure intellect. When he sees that very inscription in the Holy Fold (*Ḥaẓirat-ul-Quds*) where it had appeared first, he becomes convinced that it is the Word of God. Afterwards, it is revealed to his intellectual faculties in the form of properly arranged language through the angel.[25]

The pure intellect of the perfect prophet is extremely effective and is perpetually strengthened by the Great Manifestation (*Tajallī-i-A'ẓam*). The revelation of the Holy Qur'ān is the result of the perfection of his (the Prophet's) self and also the fulfilment of the right on the part of the Great Manifestation itself[26]

The flow of Divine Grace towards the prophet takes place in two ways. One way is of establishing a *Sharī'ah* as by this the *Sharī'ah* is revealed, and the other way is of the secret of the speech and formal specification (*Ta'yīn-i-Waḍ'ī*), as by this the Holy Qur'ān is revealed to the Prophet. Now, if the first way (namely, of the establishment of a law) precedes and hastens to assert itself, then *Ḥadīth Qudsī* is revealed, but if the second one precedes and is quick to accomplish, then it is likely it may not take place. All the Divine Books revealed before the Holy Qur'ān were revealed after the type of the *Ḥadīth Qudsī*.[27]

25. Ibid., *Saṭa'* 19. 20,

26. Ibid., *Saṭa'*, 21.

27. Ibid., *Saṭa'* 21 :

- - و کتب الاهی پیش از قرآن همه به روش حدیث قدسی بودند -

Chapter VI

THE SHARĪ'AH

SHARĪ'AH is the natural law of man, and is the result of the requirement of his species itself. When the human species reaches a particular degree of development, it demands a particular kind of *Sharī'ah*. It has not been thrust upon man against his will but has been given to him at his request. Now his good lies in obeying it, and through it he attains perfection and reaches his destined goal. The difference, which at times appears in the Laws of the various prophets, is also the result of man's specific capability. Religion (*Dīn*) is originally one and the same, and it is this same religion that all the prophets have called upon people to follow.[1]

Essentials of Religion. The essentials of a religion, which does not suffer change by the change of time, which are enshrined in the teachings of all the prophets are: belief in the unity of God, that He is one, has no equal and worship is due to Him alone, that the Judgment Day will come, and man would be made to account for his actions. These are the fundamental principles of religion (*dīn*) and they go by the name of Islam. Islam is not the name of any particular group or section. Any man irrespective of his birth, caste and creed, if he believes in God, in His Apostle,

1. *Ḥujjatullāh*, Vol. I, pp. 86-88.

has faith in the life to come, and does good deeds, then he is certainly within the bounds of Islam.[2]

Thus, all the nations and communities, in spite of their differences, can come to an agreement on one common point and meet together on one and the same platform. That common point among them is the belief in the Unity of God and the recognition of the broader principles of virtue and vice. These are the very requirements of man's angelic faculty (*Malakīyah*) which is present in every human being. It is well known that two faculties are inherent in the nature of man. One is his angelic faculty and the other is his bestial faculty. His happiness lies in strengthening the former and making it prevail upon the latter. But if his bestial faculty gains ascendancy over his angelic faculty, he grows worse and becomes wretched.

The reward or punishment in the other world depends upon the states and the conditions of man's heart, which are the result of his actions. If the specific constitution of a man is orderly and normal, and his matter is so free from defect that it does not prevent his species from making its fullest manifestation, then he will surely look upon strengthening the angelic faculty and weakening the bestial force as his real happiness, and will naturally remain in pursuit of it. He would surely be attracted towards the

2. *Al-Budūr-ul-Bāzighah*, p. 167 :

فالتجربة و الاستقراء شاهدان على ان الايمان بالله تعالى لا تخلو عنه أرض نعم قد تكون مشوبا بنحو من انحاء الشرك و كذالک العلم بمجازاة ما و بمعاد ما على خطأ او صواب ۔

Fath-ur-Raḥmān, Sūrah al-Mā'idah, verse 72.

achievement of that happiness, as the iron is attracted towards the flint. This is the very nature of man he is created after.

Saintly Persons All the people in the world, in spite of their differences in their habits, customs and systems, manners and mental attitudes, agree upon this that, besides the worldly happiness, there is another happiness as well, which is far superior and far better than the first one, and which goes to the lot of only those who have conquered their lower selves and have broken through the material world. It is so because the angelic nature is common among all of them.

Shāh Walīyullāh is of the belief that the God-fearing persons, such as the Divine Sages, and the attracted (*Majdhūb*) Sūfīs do exist in other communities as well. They have attained real happiness, but their number is very small.[3]

If one were to refer to the books of history, one will find that there are some saintly persons in every community who have made the acquisition of that happiness as their aim in life. It is, therefore, that when the rulers of time and the people of learning see them, they are convinced that these holy persons have actually achieved that happiness. Then they begin to pay homage to them and solicit their bless-

3. *Ḥujjatullāh*, Vol. I, p. 52 :

... و يكون منهم على طرف شاسع و صقع بعيد و هذا هو الذى يرومه المتألهون من الحكماء و المجذوبون من الصوفية فوصل بعضهم غاية مداها و قليل ما هم -

ings. They court their following and count a moment's association with them as a token of pride and good fortune for themselves.[4]

Sharī'ah *is the Requirement of Man's Species.* The *Sharī'ah* was imposed on man only when he required and importunately prayed for it. God, out of grace, readily met his requirement, and accepted his prayer and gave him a *Sharī'ah* which was nothing short of a boon and a blessing for him. Shāh Ṣāḥib explains the course of the imposition of Law as under: First of all you think over the plants. Look at the trees, and mark their diversity. They are of different kinds; their branches, their leaves and their fruits differ. Their smell, their colour, and the taste of their fruits, are all different. This kind of difference is the result of the plant's specific form. In other words, all the peculiarities in the plant are the product of its specific form. Now, to raise the question as to why the fruit of the palm-tree is of this kind is quite absurd. It amounts to asking the question as to why the palm-tree has been created like this. The palm-tree itself requires that its fruit should be of this kind. Like plants you look again on the animals, each one of them has a distinguishing colour and shape, but in addition to plant peculiarities, animals possess some other peculiarities as well, like voluntary movement and natural instinct. Each individual animal has been given a special Divine knowledge, which distinguishes it from the others and which is enough to guide it to fulfil its

4. Ibid., Vol. I, pp. 50-51.

needs in life. As the plants do not move with will and possess no feeling, the roots were created for them to suck the fine ingredients of water, air and earth, and then distribute them in their branches and leaves. The animals, on the other hand, have feelings and move at will; therefore, they were given a natural instinct for the satisfaction of their requirements. Apart from that, each one of them has its own way of eating, drinking and settling down. The quadrupeds eat fodder, the wild beasts feed on flesh, the birds fly and the fishes swim in the water. All this variety proceeds from their specific form, and this specific form grants each one of its individuals a particular perception and an instinctive knowledge. All the knowledge and perception of the animals are absolutely natural and instinctive, and they have nothing to do with the acquisition The case of man is, however, different. In addition to the peculiarities of animals, he has been given another kind of perception also which is acquired. With this perception, man acquires various kinds of sciences and arts. It is this perceptive faculty which makes him a king, a philosopher and an artisan, but all these branches of knowledge and perception have connection with his outward self only. Besides these, man has been given one more perception, namely, the angelic faculty. This is that very angelic faculty by means of which, while looking to the world spread around him, he begins to think of his Creator, of one who gives him subsistence. In this way he eventually comes to believe in the existence of a great power. He then bows down before it in reverence and performs all the acts of obedience. The only difference is that the acknowledgment of the other creation is by the language expressive of its condition, while that of man is by the language of the tongue. It is so because he is given the reason, and it is from the requirements of his very nature to make the expression of it in words. Against his angelic faculty there is a bestial faculty in him and both these are always at war with each other. God has, however, inspired man with the conscience of what is wrong for his self (*nafs*) and what is right for it. If he performs deeds which go to strengthen his angelic faculty, he deserves to receive a goodly reward, but if he happens to do an evil, this will lend support to his bestial faculty and he, in consequence thereof, deserves to be punished. God, out of His Grace shown to every order (*niẓām*) in the world, helps man in both the cases when he works for good or makes an attempt at evil. Thus it is man himself who, through the tongue of his capability, is pleading to his Lord to make obligatory for him what may be suitable to the angelic faculty and give him a good reward for it, and make unlawful for him what may drag him to bestiality and give him punishment for that.[5]

Thus, God gave His Law out of His sheer kindness to mankind, and it was indeed the very capability of man's species that begged for it, and it was indeed the varying condition of his species which

5. Ibid., Vol. 1, pp. 20, 21, 22, 50, 51 ; *Saṭa'āt*, *Saṭ* 5.

asked for a particular kind of *Sharī'ah* according to the requirements of the then existing conditions. Thus the argument of God is now established against him and if, after this, he questions as to why the prayer is made obligatory, why obedience to the prophet is necessary and why fornication and stealing are forbidden, the answer to these questions is that they are made obligatory or forbidden in the same way as the grazing of fodder and the eating of flesh are made obligatory and forbidden for the quadrupeds, and the eating of fodder and of flesh are made forbidden and obligatory for the wild beasts respectively. The only difference is that the animals know these sciences through natural instincts, and then follow them accordingly, while man learns them through acquisition, observation, inspiration and imitation. Consequently, whosoever will disobey that Law will deliberately harm himself.[6]

The feeling of passivity is also the effect of the spiritual power. When he (man) does some work, its impression is left on his heart. If the work done is good, he feels some sort of happiness, but if it is bad, he feels rather sad and depressed. Animals have no such feeling. Whatever acts they do, their impressions do not stay longer on their hearts, and disappear very soon The case of man is rather different. The impressions of his actions performed intentionally remain on his heart without any loss. A

6. Ibid., Vol. I, pp. 20-24 :

فتبين ان التكليف من مقتضيات النوع -

practical example of this is the occasional recollection by man of his good or bad actions even after the expiration of many years.[7]

The causes of the different *Sharī'ahs* in different ages are quite obvious. When the signs of the old *Sharī'ah* are nearly lost and no more practised and mankind is found heading towards a crisis, the new *Sharī'ah* comes to rescue the suffering humanity from further ruination. But whenever a particular *Sharī'ah* is planned for the people, due consideration is always paid both to their bodily and intellectual capabilities. All those practices which were popular and current among them and with which they were contented and satisfied are to be taken into account, as the original purpose implied in the imposition of Law is to have the maximum possible following.[8]

Human Development. The conditions of the world are changing from time to time, hence they cannot be comprised by one *Sharī'ah.* Apart from this, the mind of man is slowly and steadily developing and this development is the main cause of the change in the *Sharī'ah.* From Adam down to the times of the Prophet Idrīs (Enoch) humanity was passing through its initial stage and its development was restricted to the first *Irtifāq* (rustic life) and the people were not obliged to believe in the angels and the Hereafter. This was an age in which the sciences of medicine and astronomy were very popular, and they were true as well, though mixed up with the untrue and the

7. Ibid., p 29.

8. *Fuyūḍ-ul-Ḥaramain*, Mashhad, p 4.

original truth was blended with falsehood.[9]

Then followed the age of Prophet Noah, wherein people were very stout and strong in their physique. Accordingly, they were given a *Sharī'ah* suitable for crushing their animal vitality. Praying at night and fasting during the day were made obligatory for them and, in addition to that, other hard worship was also prescribed in order to suppress their bestiality. The Prophet Noah was the first prophet commanded by God to go and warn people against their evil acts, to order them to obey the Law, and to dispute with them for His message. His *Sharī'ah* also enjoined unity of God, observance of worship, belief in the angels, in the Divine Scriptures, in the Prophets and in the Hereafter.[10]

His age was followed by the age of Prophet Hūd and Ṣāliḥ. The people of 'Ād disobeyed their Prophet Ṣāliḥ and rebelled, and in consequence were destroyed by a violent wind which blew over them for seven consecutive days and eight nights, and this kind of punishment suited them the most, because they had their settlements in the sandy lands, and the weather of that area was dry and hot; as such, a punishment in the form of a violent wind was the most appropriate.[11]

In the period that preceded Prophet Ibrāhīm,

9. *Ta'wil-ul-Aḥādith*, p.14 ; *Tafhmiāt*, Vol. I, p. 68 ; Vol, II, pp 71-72
ففي الدورة الاولى كان المجازاة لا يتوقف على معرفة البعث بعد الموت ولا الملائكة .

10 *Ta'wil 4l-Aḥādith*, pp. 15-16 ; *Tafhimāt*, Vol. I, p. 68 ; Vol II, p 71.

11 *Tā'wil-ul-Aḥadith*, pp 16-17.

the worship of the sun and stars prevailed, and the people used to raise buildings for worship in their names. They believed that whosoever entered them became the favourite of the stars for which they were raised. According to their belief, the light of the Divine Science had fallen upon the stars and the face of the Creator had appeared reflected in the mirror of Nature. Thus, the worship of the objects of Nature formed the basis of their religion : as they were of view that no concentration of thought on any immaterial object was conceivable, unless there was fixed for it some direction.[12]

Then came the age of the Prophet Ibrāhīm (Abraham) who was very much inclined towards *Fitrah* (Nature). He rose up to end the worship of stars, fire and idols. He proclaimed the unity of God and laid the foundation of His worship. He completely changed the outlook of his people. The human heart now became the manifestation of Divinity and the seat of its sciences, and this was known as *Ḥanafīyyah* (true religion), the speciality of his age. He was followed by the Prophets Lot, Yūsuf (Joseph), Ayyūb (Job), Shu'aib (Jethro), Dāwūd (David) and Sulaimān (Solomon) in succession. The Prophet Dāwūd was skilled in state administration and in the rule of the country. He fixed the limits of religion, waged wars against the unbelievers and was an expert in solving difficult problems. But all these prophets were, however, wanting in caliphate.

12. *Fuyūḍ-ul-Ḥaramain*, Mashhad, p. 4; *Tafhīmāt*, Vol. II, pp. 71-72; *Ilhām-ur-Raḥmān*, p. 116.

Their age was followed by that of the Prophet Moses. He was a great knower of the Divine Sciences and was of a very high rank, as his prophecy (partially) included caliphate as well. He warned people against their evil actions by citing to them the examples of the past people who had suffered terrible punishment because of their disobedience to God.[13]

When Jesus came, he introduced some leniency in his *Sharī'ah.* Some things which were previously unlawful for people were rendered lawful for them. The teachings of the Proohet Moses could not spread farther than the Isrā'īl community; while the Prophet Jesus, no doubt, attempted at the dissemination of his teachings among other peoples as well, but unfortunately he himself was disowned as an authority even by his own men, the Israelites.[14]

Lastly came the Holy Prophet Muḥammad, who was, however, distinguished from the rest by his virtue of being both the perfect Prophet and the perfect Caliph. The *Sharī'ah* brought by him is unique inasmuch as it is exceedingly clear, well grounded, unambiguous and simple, very easy to profess and practise and is absolutely free from any confusion. It is so clear in its arguments that the question of any further clearness does not arise. Besides, it is the only *Sharī'ah* in which the limits of the payment of *Zakāt* (almsgiving) are fixed. It is superior to all other religions as it does not consist only what other prophets brought individually but something more as

13. *Ta'wil-ul-Aḥādith,* pp. 17-23, 32-45 ; *Tafhimāt,* Vol. II, p. 166.
14. *Ta'wil-al-Aḥādith,* p. 59 ; *Ilhām-ur-Raḥmān,* pp. 12-13.

well. The verse: "Today We have perfected your religion for you and have completed My favour on you"[15] had never been revealed to any prophet before, nor its revelation was proper for any but the Holy Prophet Muḥammad, as he has not kept concealed any philosophy, any item of guidance, any knowledge and any secret, but has given it out clearly or allusively. After him there is none so perfect as to tell what he has not told.[16]

Religion is One. All these are the stages of the development of man's mind. As it went on developing it used to receive a fresh law according to its requirements. Religion remained essentially the same, but it changed only its form and shape in the light of the change of times. All religions, despite different form and shape, agree upon the basic articles of faith and the fundaments of virtue. For example, every religion that has come down from God prescribes purity, prayer, fasts, almsgiving and the pilgrimage. It is, however, a different matter if the methods of the observance of these duties be dissimilar. To seek the nearness of God through prayer and worship is the teaching of every religion. The remembrance of God in the morning and in the evening for which the word *Dhikr* has come, reading of the Divine Scriptures and reckoning it as a means of a goodly reward are enshrined in every religion. Similarly, in

15. Sūrah al-Mā'idah, verse 3.

16. *Al-Budūr-ul-Bāzighah*, p. 201 ; *Tafhīmāt*, Vol. II, p. 113 :

- - و اختص نبينا صلعم دون سواه بمنقبة اعظم منها و هى أنه دخل كماله فى خلافته .

all the *Sharī'ahs*, marriage is made lawful and adultery is forbidden. It is the teaching of all the prophets that whatever government be in existence, it should follow the path of justice and equity, and safeguard the interests of the weak and give proper punishment to the criminal and the wrongdoer. It is also a duty imposed on every prophet to wage war against the opponents of the Law (*Sharī'ah*) and preach and propagate the message of God. These are the fundamental principles of religion common among all the systems of faith and worship.[17]

However, the course followed by the prophets in their teachings is not to divert people all at once to those reforms with which they were not the least acquainted, but rather teach them what they were already familiar with. For affairs like marriage, divorce, mutual dealings, judgment and punishment, the *Sharī'ah* has not suggested any new rules hitherto unknown to them. On the contrary, many current practices were allowed to continue with a slight change and replacement where necessary. Even in the case of worship and adoration, the same manners and ways were retained intact. Only those changes and inequities were abolished which the pagans had introduced in the true religion. Principles of worship and the observance of its appointed times were given a systematic treatment in the new Dispensation (Islam) and every form of worship was exclusively reserved for God. The main cause of the advent of the prophets

17. *Ḥujjatullāh*, Vol. 1, pp. 68, 86-87.

is to teach people the worship of God, and to suggest them some guiding principles for doing worldly things correctly. It is, therefore, that the Holy Prophet has said: "I have been raised to perfect the virtues of character."[18]

It is a known fact that the *Sharī'ahs* of the prophets have differed due to certain causes and expediencies. The injunctions of the *Sharī'ah* had to pay due consideration to them. For example, when the people of the Prophet Noah were physically strong andsturdy, the fasting during the day was prescribed for them in order to suppress the fury of their animal power. But as the followers of Prophet Muhammad were constitutionally weak, they were absolved of the observance of the continuous fasts. In like manner, the property acquired through booty was not made lawful for the people in the past, but had been made lawful for those who came after them because of their weakness. According to the Law of Moses, Jerusalem was the direction fixed for offering prayer, while the followers of Prophet Muhammad were asked to turn their faces towards the Ka'bah. In the Mosaic Law, the penalty for intentional murder was retaliation, but in the Islamic Law fine is also allowed (provided the heirs of the murdered be contented with that).[19]

Man Responsible for Change of Revelation. Here below is cited an example which will show how far the mentality of the people is responsible for the re-

18. Ibid., Vol. I, pp. 68, 86-87; *al-Fauz-ul-Kabīr*, pp. 7-9.
19. *Ḥujjatullāh*, Vol. I, pp. 87, 90; *Tafhimāt*, Vol. II, p. 23.

velation of a particular Divine injunction. The verse of the Qur'ān reads: "All food was lawful for the children of Isrā'īl except what Isrā'īl had forbidden for himself before the revelation of the Pentateuch. Say, Bring Pentateuch, then recite it if you are truthful."[20] The story in this connection runs as follows: Once the Prophet Ya'qūb (Jacob) fell ill. He made a vow that if God cured him he will not eat throughout his life the thing he liked most. When he was cured, he gave up eating the flesh of the camel and the milk of the she-camel or, in other words, he forbade these things for himself, as both of them were to his utmost taste and choice. After his death, his children also, in imitation of his practice, abandoned their use. This state of affairs continued for centuries together with the result that it became settled in the minds of Banū Isrā'īl that whosoever from among them will make use of them will be committing a crime. Accordingly, taking their mentality into consideration there came a prohibitory order in the revelation of the Pentateuch.

When the Prophet Muhammad came and declared himself as the follower of Ibrāhīm (Abraham), the Jews at once reacted, and questioned that if his claim to the obedience of the practice of Ibrāhīm (Abraham) was right, then why he was eating the flesh of the camel. God clarifying the actual position said that the flesh of the camel was forbidden for the Jews because of the mental tendency that they had developed and it was merely a temporary measure. The Prophet Muhammad descended from the Bunū Ismā'īl who

20. Sūrah Āl-i-'Imrān, verse 93.

were free from that belief, therefore, the original injunction of the religion of Ibrāhīm was retained and the previous one revealed only for the time being and that also due to a certain reason was withdrawn. From this it has become crystal clear that the religion (*dīn*) in spirit and substance is one and the same and it is man himself who is the cause of that little bit of change which has come in its form and shape in the course of time.[21]

So long as man is in this world, he will continue to be the target of its temptations. Its frequent deceptions, and those of his lower self, coupled with his incomplete knowledge of God, have encompassed him from all sides. The veils of all these three (the veil of nature [*Tabī'ah*], the veil of custom and the veil of the bad knowledge about God) which are his open enemies have wholly or partially covered him, and the prophets, as a matter of fact, came one after another, with the sole purpose of removing them.

Necessity of Islam. The causes that necessitated the emergence of a new religion (Islam) which abrogated all other religions, according to Shāh Walīyullāh, are as follows.

When injustice and wrongdoing became widespread, the signs of truth and righteousness were no more visible and the Divine Laws were tampered with, the advent of an *Imām* became inevitable, so that he may deal with the people who were heading towards

21. *Ḥujjatullāh*, Vol. I, p. 88 : *Fatḥ-ur-Raḥmān*, Sūrah 'Āl-i-'Imrān, verse 93.

their destruction, as an orthodox caliph deals with unjust rulers. God sent his Prophet Muḥammad, whose duty it was to make an effort to bring all the people the world over to accept the new faith. But for the performance of this hard job he had to adopt some new methods. First of all he had to create a party of his own, and then chalk out a programme to proceed with When that was done he used that party as a tool in his hand for the execution of his mission and spread its members throughout the world for the fulfilment of his object. It is so, because the life of a prophet is not so long, nor is it the work of a single person to deal with different peoples and countries. He has to bring with himself such *Sharī ah* which could serve as a natural religion for the people. In other words, his *Sharī'ah* should be to the requirement of their nature, simple and easy to accept and practise. What may characterise the new religion is firstly to give preference to the treatment of the habits and the ways of life of the people of the country in which the Law-giver was himself born; secondly, to those of the other peoples with a view to cleansing their hearts and reforming their character. The new faith, however, should not prescribe for them hard rules and rigid practices. Again, it is very necessary to make all the people follow that Law (*Sharī'ah*), because it is impossible to prepare separate Law for every community. To make a detailed study of the sciences and the habits of every people and then form a Law in the light of the information gathered is not possible. If the people are unable even to preserve the traditions of the *Sharī'ah* which they follow, then to preserve and look after the teachings and traditions of all the *Sharī'ahs* is a sheer impossibility. It will not also be proper that the case of every Law be left over to the followers and the learned men of that Law, because by so doing the very purpose of the new faith (*Sharī'ah*) would be defeated. Then it may be borne in mind that the work of such a magnitude cannot be completed speedily and needs a long period for its completion. If the history of the great religions like Judaism, Christianity and Islam be taken into consideration, it will be found that in the beginning only a handful of persons turned up to embrace them, then slowly and gradually the adherents of all these three became powerful nations.[22]

Islam is the last religion and the one acceptable to God He wishes that Islam alone should remain as the religion of man, and that it should have prevalence over all other religions. Consequently if a man does not embrace it, he is definitely going against His wish and incurs His anger. And whosoever will work against it will certainly be the loser. Indeed, the good of man lies in making Islam his own religion.[23]

The reason is that if we take it for granted that there are some Jews and Christians still adhering

22. *Ḥujjatullāh*, Vol. I, pp. 117-19.
23. *Al-Budūr-ul-Bāzighah*, p. 191.

to the upright religion (*Dīn Ḥanīfī*) and they have not mixed up anything in that religion, and thus it is not necessary for them to enter into the religion brought by Muḥammad and adopt his religion and acknowledge his mission from the side of their perfecting themselves and their drawing near to God, even then it is obligatory on them to accept Islam from the other side. And that side is that when God intended to bring upright religion by the fourth phase of the socio-economic development and is pleased with it, then any diversion from it amounts to His disobedience, opposition, curse and farness from His mercy. The pleasure and the approval of God is confined to the obedience to the religion brought by Muḥammad and to the open acknowledgment of his mission.[24]

Prevalence of Islam. In giving explanation of the verse : "It is He Who sent His messenger with guidance and the true religion; so that He should make it prevail upon all other religions, even though the infidels do not like,"[25] Shāh Ṣāḥib says that the religion of Islam did not acquire complete prevalence over other religions in the lifetime of the Holy Prophet, because the Christians and the Jews were still in power. It is for this reason that many commentators have been confused while explaining this verse properly. Ḍaḥḥāk,[26] for example, is of view that the complete

24. *Al-Budūr-ul-Bāzighah*, pp. 199-200.

25. Sūrah al-Barā'at, verse 33.

26. Ḍaḥḥāk b. Muzāḥim of Kūfah was a famous commentator, a traditionist and a grammarian. He died in 105/723 at Merv.

prevalence will take practical shape when Jesus would reappear. Husain b Faḍl[27] in his comments opines that by the complete prevalence is meant the prevalence of argument and proof. Imām Shāfi'ī's explanation is rather weightier. He says that Islam achieved prevalence over other religions in the sense that the Holy Prophet explained in details to those who listened to him what the truth was. Besides, Islam prevailed in another way also. In those days the polytheists were of two kinds : the People of the Book and the illiterate. The illiterate were so dominated that they embraced Islam ; while the People of the Book were reduced to a state to pay the tribute (*Jizyah*) with lowliness, and thus came under the application of the Law of Islam.

In this connection he observes that wherever a difficulty in understanding the meaning of a certain verse were to appear, two points should be borne in mind. One is to weigh the words of the Qur'ān in the balance of pure reason against the meaning given to it by the people. If both of them be found in conformity with each other, well and good, otherwise one should give up that interpretation. The other point is that we should consult the Tradition of the Holy Prophet and take it as our guide, because the Holy Prophet is the real commentator of the Qur'ān. Now, when we put that prevalence which the Prophet achieved over Christians of Najrān, the Magians

27. Ḥusain b. Faḍl was a great commentator and a worshipping devotee. He died in 282/895 when he was 104 years old.

of Ḥajar and the Jews of Khyber (and in consequence of which they paid *Jizyah* and tax) in one pan of the balance and the words of the Qur'ān "so that He should prevail it upon all other religions" in its other pan, we do not find any equilibrium whatsoever between the two. A prevalence over a few of the People of the Book cannot be equal to a prevalence over all the religions. The meaning of the complete prevalence is that, excepting Islam, all other religions be made powerless, their supporters and missionaries be divided and broken up and Islam alone be found dominating and glorious.

As for the Tradition in reference to the prevalence of Islam, the Prophet is reported to have said: "God folded up the earth for me, and I saw clearly its east and west, and, verily, the sovereignty of my community will extend to the portion folded for me and I was given the treasures of gold and silver." According to another report, his saying is: "Chosroes perished, and now no other Chosroes will appear again and Caesar will certainly perish and after him there will be no other Caesar and you will distribute their wealth in the way of God." Again, on one occasion he had said that "No house or tent will remain on the surface of the earth but that God will make Islam enter therein." From these Traditions it appears that the complete prevalence of Islam will take place after the death of the Holy Prophet.

If the pronoun implied in *li-yuẓhirahū* (ليظهره) be taken as referring to the guidance (*al-hudā*) and the true religion (*dīn-il-ḥaqq*), then the meaning would be that the sending of the Prophet with guidance and true religion will be the cause of prevalence. In this respect it is not necessary that the prevalence aimed at be achieved during his lifetime. His advent itself became the cause of prevalence even though it was brought about by his lieutenants after him. Again, if the pronoun in *li-yuẓhirahū* were to refer to the Holy Prophet, even then the meaning remains unchanged, as the prevalence of the true religion achieved by his lieutenants is in reality counted as his own achievement.

In short, the world in those days was divided under the rule of two emperors, the Chosroes and the Caesar. The kingdom of Chosroes extended as far as Iraq, Yemen, Khurāsān, Tūrān, Turkestan, Zāwilistān and Bakhtar. The inhabitants of those countries were Magians (fire-worshippers). Transoxania and India were also obeying the king of Persia and paid taxes to him. Rome and the provinces around it, Egypt, Morocco and Africa, were under the yoke of the Caesar, the Roman emperor. The people of those regions were Christians. The religion of both the Chosroes and the Caesar was *Ibāḥat* (liberty, licentiousness, that is to say, to do whatever one may like) which had dominated all other religions. They both, by their words and deeds, were attracting people towards this religion, and were the chief cause of its propagation. Other religions, like Judaism, Hinduism and Sabianism were very weak in comparison to them and their followers were without unity and discipline. Thus, to crush both these powers and achieve domination over them, in reality, amounted to world domination.

Here it is necessary to note that the word *li-yuẓhirahū* signifies that the guidance and the true religion, with which the Prophet was sent, would be predominant, clear and well known, and not suppressed and concealed. It also has been the Divine Wish that the prevalence of Islam should continue without a break in every age.[28]

Continuation of Jihād. From the above explanation as given by Shāh Sāhib it has become clear that *Jihād* is permanent and continuous, but by *Jihād* is not meant an actual warfare at all times. To keep oneself ready and well prepared, and to make all the necessary provisions for self-defence is an absolute necessity. The nation which is afraid of fighting is indeed not worth living. From the prevalence of Islam Shāh Ṣāḥib seems to mean the political prevalence (combined with moral and economic prevalence), because the domination of Islam could not otherwise be insured.

The movement towards the achievement of this prevalence should at no time be allowed to slacken or stop. The verse applies to us in no less degree than it applied to the people of the distant past. *Jihād* of

28. *Izālat-ul-Khafā'*, Vol. I, pp. 44-66 :

و معنی آیت هو الذی آنست که هدی و دین حق که آنحضرت صلعم بآن مرسل بودند ظاهر و غالب باشد و جلی و مشهور نه مخفی و مستور - - - پس مراد ظهور دین حق است قرنا بعد قرن -

course will have different forms according to the requirements of the conditions, but the lukewarmness which we have shown towards the achievement of the prevalence of Islam is indeed tantamount to our not fulfilling the Wish of God, and we cannot, as such, escape the grave consequences resulting from our indifference, apathy and negligence towards this most sacred duty of *Jihād*.

Chapter VII

THE POLITICS

SHĀH 'Abd-ur-Raḥīm, the father of Shāh Walīyullāh, lived at the time when the reign of Aurangzeb 'Ālamgīr was at the peak of its glory. 'Ālamgīr's empire was very vast and powerful. The Emperor himself was a pious and God-fearing person, but, in spite of it, the Hindus and the Shī'ites were rather harassed. This policy of the government subsequently became the cause of its downfall. The hostile and the disgruntled elements were hard at work against it, with the result that the Mughal Empire, immediately after his death, began to decline so much so that in the lifetime of Shāh Walīyullāh alone no less than ten rulers succeeded the throne one after another.[1]

Shāh 'Abd-ur-Raḥīm saw all this happening before his eyes and, though he had a hand in the preparation of *Fatāwā'-i-'Ālamgīrī*, he was not of the *'Ulamā'* of the Royal Court, and was a man of derwish nature. He was, however, unable to do anything in practice against the government, but did this much at least that he gave away all the knowledge he possessed to his worthy son.

Shāh Walīyullāh was the acknowledged reformer of his time and the work begun by Mujaddid Alif

1. Shāh Walīyullāh was born in the year 1114/1702, four years before the death of Aurangzeb 'Ālamgīr.

Thānī was successfully completed by him. He, however, accepted him as his precursor. He carefully watched the gradual decline of the empire and the disintegration of the Muslim community which was losing ground everywhere. This led him to seriously think over the matter and try to find out some solution to save the country from collapse But before giving any practical shape to his contemplated scheme, he considered it proper to visit the holy lands, so as to complete his study of the Tradition.[2]

Thus, he left for the Hejaz in 1143/1731 and, after a stay of over a year there, he on his return to India found that the existing order had become out of date and needed to be replaced. The first step, therefore, which he took was the translation of the Holy Qur'ān into Persian with brief commentary notes. This in a way was the preliminary step towards his political movement. Persian in those days was the language of the masses and, to address them, the Persian version of the Qur'ān was necessary, and his brief commentary of it proved to be very useful in explaining the object of the Qur'ān.[3]

During the days of Shams-ul-Hind, Shāh 'Abd-ul-'Azīz, the eldest son of Shāh Walīyullāh, Urdu had taken the place of Persian; therefore, his brother Shāh 'Abd-ul-Qādir translated the Holy Qur'ān into Urdu, and his nephew Shāh Ismā'īl Shahīd wrote

2. *Maktūbāt.*
3. *Muqaddimah-i-Fatḥ-ur-Raḥmān, Fuyūḍ- ul- Ḥaramain,* Mashhad, p. 40:
- - - وسألونى ماذا حكم الله فى هذا الساعة ؟ قلت فك كل نظام -

some religious books in that language. As the movement started by Shāh Ṣāḥib was for the masses who were to be trained according to the programme chalked out by him, these preliminary measures of rendering religious literature into their language were taken. But here it is worthy to note that Shāh Walīyullāh, for all his activities whether religious or political, always keeps the Qur'ān before himself as his guide. He derives inspiration from it, and does not turn to any other source as far as possible. The life of the Holy Prophet was sufficient for him to solve his difficulties, as he was the correct interpreter of the Qur'ānic teachings. He had laid the foundation of his political movement on this verse of the Qur'ān: "Have they not seen that We are reducing the earth from all its sides."[4]

Establishment of Islamic Government in Mecca. It is an undeniable fact, he says, that the government of Islam was established in Mecca before migration and it was quite an independent one, even though it was not so powerful as to use force and begin with aggression. Against the opinion of the majority of the commentators and historians, who have linked the beginning of the Islamic State with the advent of the Holy Prophet to Medina (as if in their opinion the social life of the Muslims in Mecca had no political character behind), Shāh Ṣāhib considered this verse as a Meccan revelation, and, by so doing, he has left no room for anyone to question the policy of

4. Sūrah Ra'd, verse 41.

the Holy Prophet. Some non-Muslim writers in their writings have made the charge that so long as the Prophet was in Mecca, he was merely a preacher, but as soon as he came to Medina he turned out to be the ruler of a state.

Shāh Ṣāḥib, while explaining the verse mentioned above, states that the power of Islam went on increasing in Arabia day by day, and the enemies' territory continued diminishing gradually, as many Arab tribes that time, like Ghifār, Juhainah, Muzainah, and some tribes of the Yemen had embraced Islam. On that account, the power of the enemy decreased considerably. All these changes had taken place while the Holy Prophet was still there in Mecca. This shows that the Islamic government was established in Mecca, but, of course, in principle the movement was non-violent. According to it (non-violence), the people were to be reformed, improved and won over through preaching and exhortation.[5]

This is the very reason why in Mecca the invitation of the Holy Prophet to accept Islam was confined to the polytheists only. But when he came to Medina and Islam gathered force, it became no more necessary for him to abide by the principles of non-violence. Accordingly, he began to call upon the People of the Book for the first time (as they were never called upon before migration) towards the acceptance of the new faith, but they did not like it

5. *Fatḥ-ur-Raḥmān*, Sūrah Ra'd, verse 41 ; *Tafhimāt*, Vol. I, pp. 12-13.

and rose up in opposition against him.

Political Conditions and Sack of Delhi. The chaotic order in the state administration and the worsening of the political conditions during the days of Shāh Walīyullāh bear testimony to the fact that during the reign of Aḥmad Shāh (1161-1168/1748-1754), the army was not paid its salary for full three years. Shākir Khān Pānīpatī writes that a list of the articles of the Royal palace was prepared and passed on to the shopkeepers for their sale so as to make up the payment.[6]

Marhattas, Sikh, Jat and Rohilla tribes were very unruly and oppressive. At every time they disturbed peace, caused anxiety to the government and harmed the Muslims frequently. So weak was the position of the government that the rule of Sulṭān Shāh 'Ālam was limited only to the outskirts of Delhi. The luxurious living of the rulers was indeed an apt illustration of that of the days of Chosroes and Caesar. But for these principal vices, there were other causes as well, namely, the limitation of the reserved territory, bankruptcy of the state exchequer, multiplicity of the *Jāgīrdārs* and the monopoly system. In short, the storm of misfortunes had started blowing from every side and, for all this, the upper class was mainly responsible which, for the sake of its ease and comfort, was sucking the blood of its poor subjects. This was the then condition of Delhi the capital of

6. Khaliq Aḥmad Niẓāmī, *Waliyullāh Dehlavi Key Siyāsi Maktūbāt*, p. 162.

the empire.[7]

Soon after his return from *Haramain* (Mecca and Medina) where he stayed for fourteen months, in the year 1146/1733, Delhi was ransacked by Nādir Shāh in 1150/1737. India received such a crushing defeat at the hands of Nādir that the like of it cannot be found in history. Delhi lay exposed to the pillage and savagery of Nādir and the atrocities committed by the invading hordes went to such an extent that respectable families had made up their minds to perform *Jauhar* (setting oneself on fire). Shāh Ṣāḥib, however, used to prevent them from doing so by narrating to them the story of Imām Ḥusain. In fact, some twenty years before the devastation of Delhi in the year 1131/1719 after the cruel murder of Prince Farrukh-Sair, the country had turned into a veritable hell. There was no security and no order anywhere.[8]

Caliphate. While throwing light upon the nature of caliphate, he has made clear references to the ruling clique, from which it appeared that, apart from the political instability, the Muslim government of that time had neglected religion also. About caliphate, he says: "There is a group which takes caliphate in the sense of *Imāmah* and considers that the necessary qualifications of a caliph are that he should be a Hāshimid, a Fāṭimid, and an infallibe one. As a matter of fact, by caliphate is meant the government

7. *Al-Budūr-ul-Bāzighah*, p. 137; *Ḥujjatullāh*, Vol. I, p. 105:
وما تراه من ملوک بلاذک یغنیک عن حکایاتهم (قیصر و کسرٰی) ـ
8. *Anfās-ul-'Ārifīn*, p. 87: *Malfūẓāt-i-Shāh 'Abd-ul-'Azīz*,

of the Muslims. No sensible man can apply this meaning to the twelve caliphs (*Ithnā' 'Asharah*) with the exception of Ḥaḍrat 'Alī. Caliphate, even according to the *Sharī'ah*, is the government by means of which, while fulfilling the duty of a lieutenant of the Holy Prophet, arrangements are to be made for the maintenance of religion. If a man is not a ruler nor are his orders executed, then he, in that case, is not a caliph, even if he be superior to the whole of the community and be a Fāṭimid and a sinless one. Similarly, if an unbeliever happens to be the ruler or there is a government under which cases are decided not according to the Law (*Sharī'ah*), but at the point of the sword, and the ruler is concerned only with the collection of revenues, and takes no interest in the affairs of the religion, like the carrying of Holy War, enforcement of the penal laws and the disposal of cases according to it (Religion), then he cannot be the caliph. Such is the case of our present-day rulers."[9]

In order to give practical shape to his programme Shāh Ṣāḥib formed an executive committee which, through teachings and guidance, used to publicise this revolutionary movement among the Sūfīs and the *'Ulamā'* on the one hand, and the rulers and the chiefs on the other hand Maulānā Muḥammad 'Āshiq,

9. *Izālat-ul-Khafā'*, Vol. I, p. 256 :

- - - در شرع مراد از وی (خلافت) پادشاهی است برای تصدی اقامت دین محمدی صلعم به نیابت آنحضرت صلعم پس اگر کسے پادشاه نباشد و حکم او نافذ نبود خلیفه نیست هر چند فرض کنیم که او افضل امت باشد و معصوم و مفترض الطاعة و فاطمی - - -

Maulawī Nūrullāh Budhānawī and Maulānā Muhammad Amīn Kashmīrī in particular were the leading members of the committee, and its branches were established in different parts of the country; for example, the Madrasah at Najībābād, Dā'irah-i-Shāh 'Ālamullāh at Rā'i Barellī, and the Madrasah of Mullā Muḥammad Mu'īn-ud-Dīn at Thattā in Sind, with whom Shāh 'Abd-ul-Laṭīf of Bhit had special connections. The wide acceptance which the invitation of Shāh Walīyullāh received at the hands of the public is evident from the fact that Sulṭān Muḥammad Shāh reserved a whole quarter (Muhallah) of Jahānābād exclusively for his Madrasah, which formerly was located in a small house in Old Delhi.[10]

It is also a fact that at his instance and advice, Najīb-ud-Daulah who happened to be his faithful disciple had sent for Aḥmad Shāh Abdālī from Qandhār, who gave a crushing defeat to the Marhattas at Pānīpat. But, unfortunately, the government at Delhi had become so weak that it could not derive any advantage from it. This much, however, happened that the headmen and chiefs posted at various places became independent masters there, and, thus, started the period of petty kingdoms.[11]

Shāh Ṣāḥib's Letters to Aḥmad Shāh Abdālī and Others. Here below are given the extracts of letters Shāh Sāhib had addressed to Ahmad Shāh Abdālī for the invasion of India, with a pitiful appeal to under-

10. Maulānā 'Ubaidullāh Sindhī, *Shāh Waliyullāh aur Un kī Siyāsī Taḥrīk*, pp. 175-79.

11. Ibid., p. 57.

take this expedition, and the letters he had written to other Amīrs and chiefs. From all these, the reader will have an idea of the political, social and economic conditions of the Muslims of the eighteenth century.

An extract from a letter to Aḥmad Shāh Abdālī:

"At present there is no one more powerful and dignified king than you. It is your duty to make for India, so as to break the power of the Marhattas and rescue the helpless Muslims held in bondage by the unbelievers."[12]

At another place he in his appeal to him writes:

"I seek refuge with God against the evil done by Nādir Shāh. He, after having wiped out the Muslims and carrying loot and plunder, left the Marhattas and the Jats untouched and returned, with the result that the enemies gathered more force and the Muslim army was subdued, and the empire of Delhi became a children's play."[13]

Contents of his letter to Najīb-ud-Daulah:

"The overthrow of both the Marhattas and the Jats has been decided in the 'Court of heaven' (*al-Malā'-ul-A'lā*), until and unless the Marhattas, Jats and Sikhs are completely vanquished, no ruler will continue to remain on his throne in peace and security. In war with the enemies, sometimes one wins and sometimes loses, but on that account one need not feel worried."[14]

Besides, he had written a lengthy letter to Aḥmad Shāh Abdālī wherein he had apprised him of the true conditions of India, and had supplied him all the necessary information about its geography and historical background with a view to encouraging him to undertake military expedition to crush the enemy forces with minimum suffering and to avert the pos-

12. Khalīq Aḥmad Nizāmī, *Shāh Walīyullāh aur Un hey Siyāsi Maktūbāt*, p. 15.

13. Ibid., p. 52.

14. Ibid., pp. 32, 61, and 64.

sible destruction of the Muslims who were in minority, at the time of an attack. In its end, he had quoted a verse of the Qur'ān, which is enough to speak of his political diplomacy and his farsightedness. That verse which referred to the Truce of Ḥudaibīyah is this:

"Had there not been believing men and believing women whom you did not know that you were trampling down and on whose account a crime would have accrued to you without your knowledge. . . ."[15]

Some contents of that lengthy letter:

"Whenever there is any apprehension of a danger to the life and property of the Muslims, the Divine Wisdom desires some delay. It is the reason that Mecca was conquered after two years, because if it had been invaded at the time of the truce, a handful of the Muslims living amongst the enemy, who was in an absolute majority, would have been ruined during the attack of the Muslims. In the truce of Ḥudaibīyah and the conquest of Mecca there is a wonderful lesson of wisdom for the prudent rulers to learn, namely, where Muslims and non-Muslims be living together, due patience and forbearance must be shown Further, the enemies who have dominated the Muslims be first divided and dispersed some way and then the Muslims will automatically rally round the just ruler."[16]

"It has come in the Tradition that, in the eyes of God, destruction of the whole world is better than the unjust murder of a single Muslim. When the strong forces reach a place of mixed population, it is proper that the organising officers be posted to evacuate the Muslim population living in small villages and rehabilitate them in big towns, and then arrangement be made to give guarantee for the preservation of their honour and property."[17]

15. Sūrah al-Fatḥ, verse 25.
16. Khalīq Aḥmad Niẓāmī, *Shāh Waliyullāh aur Un key Siyāsī Maktūbāt*, pp. 54-55.
17. Ibid., pp. 53-54.

Aḥmad Shāh Abdālī invaded India nine times. Seven invasions were made during the lifetime of Shāh Walīyullāh himself. His sixth invasion took place in 1173-74/1760-61 at the invitation of Shāh Walīyullāh, Najīb-ud-Daulah the Prime Minister, and other influential personages. Whether Ahmad Shāh Abdālī possessed the requisite qualifications of a ruler according to Shāh Walīyullāh or not, this game had, however, to be played to break the rising power of the enemy for the time being. Herein lies the success of Shāh Walīyullāh. The battle of Pānīpat had changed the course of Indian history for ever.

Bengal was the target of the Britishers, and the East India Company was busy since a long time to capture political power. The Sikhs wielded such a considerable influence over the province of the Punjab that even the shrine of Sirhand did not remain safe from their loot and plunder. The continuous attacks of the Rohillas and the pillaging by the Jat tribes had wrought havoc in the country. More regrettable and tragic, above all, was the role played by the aristocrats and the high officials who were both unworthy and selfish.[18]

A little before the death of Shāh Ṣāḥib, Najaf 'Alī Khān, the fanatic Shī'ah, came in full power. He was the last Minister of the Mughal Court. In his days the marriages of the royal family members were made with the Shī'ah Sayyids of Lucknow, who wrongfully troubled and penalised many men of

18. Mirzā Maẓhar Jānjānān, *Maktūbāt* (*Kalimāt-i-Ṭayyibāt*) pp. 50-51., 61.

learning.[19]

Here the question arises that when conditions were so unfavourable and disheartening, what was the political programme of Shāḥ Sāhib and what was the true pattern of his movement? We are of opinion that, Shāh Ṣāḥib's anxiety and efforts that time were to see the central authority vested in the hands of Muslims, and their government so reformed as to give no cause of complaint to the non-Muslims. He no doubt performed a great political feat by inviting Aḥmad Shāh Abdālī to break the power of the Marhattas, but his intention was that the Muslims and non-Muslims should remain on good terms, in peace and amity, so that the rule of the Muslims may continue. Openly, of course, he could not do anything, but through Najīb-ud-Daulah he did whatever he could do to bring about reformation and improvement in the administrative machinery of the then government.

All the writings of Shāh Ṣāḥib, if thoughtfully read, will be found replete with the spirit of *Jihād*. It is indeed a matter of great regret that people that time did not listen to him.[20]

It is necessary here to remove a misunderstanding. Some people are under the wrong impression that Shāh Ṣāḥib wanted to revive the age of Akbar A'ẓam, but it is absolutely incorrect and is without foundation. The Godlessness of Akbar had no place whatsoever in the teachings of Shāh Walīyullāh. The religious

19. Ibid., p. 45 ; *Muqaddimah, al-Khair-ul-Kathir*, pp. 6-7.
20. *Tafhimāt*, Vol. II, p. 200: *Ḥujjatullāh*, Vol. II, p. 171.

dye he was dyed with can be seen from his following words:

> "We have come here in India as strangers. We take pride in our Arab origin and the Arabic language. It behoves us to stick to Arab customs and habits and should never adopt the customs and practices of the non-Arabs and the Hindus."[21]

His assertion somewhere that at present he is the lieutenant of the Prophet Yūsuf (Joseph) points out the fact that, just as Prophet Yūsuf in the capacity of a minister under 'Azīz of Egypt, had transformed the whole government machinery into Islamic type, and the infidel ruler was left only in name, in like manner he could also work upon the same formula and establish such an order in the foreign rule.[22]

Shāh Ṣāḥib, however, had visualised the fall of the government, and he, therefore, took the Meccan life of the Prophet as his guide. His movement, as has been already mentioned, was secret, under which a party was formed the duty of which was to start and carry out the missionary work throughout the country.

Open and Secret Caliphate. In religion, besides a group of open caliphs, there is a party of secret caliphs

21. *Waṣiyyat Nāmah*, pp. 11-12; *Anfās-ul-'Ārifīn*, p. 160:
این فقیر از بعض احفاد شیخ عبدالغنی مذکور استماع نمود که وی رحمة الله عالم و متورع بود و جلال‌الدین اکبر بادشاه او را مفخم و معظم داشتی و بعد از آنکه بادشاه الحاد و زندقه پیش گرفت آن رشتهٔ الفت از هم گسست ۔ تنفر تمام از هر دو جالب بظهور پیوست ۔

22. *Tafhīmāt*, Vol. II, p. 68:
و کنت یومئذ نائب یوسف علیه السلام لأنه هوالذی خلصت له الحکمة ۔

as well, and Shāh Ṣāḥib was put in charge of the secret caliphate. The job of the secret caliph is to teach people the Qur'ān, the Tradition and the *Sharī'ah* and to command them to do good and shun evil. The difference between the secret and the open caliphs is that in the case of the former no dispute arises among them, however large their number be, while contrary is the case in the latter. It is one of the responsibilities of a secret caliph to send missionaries abroad to universalise his message. This is a fact that the Holy Prophet used to send his agents to different parts of the country so as to propagate the new faith among various tribes. For example, he deputed Abū Mūsā Ash'arī to the Ash'ar tribe, Abū Dharr Ghifārī to the tribes of Aslam and Ghifār, 'Umar b. Murrah to the tribe of Jahainah, 'Āmir al-Ḥaḍramī to the tribe of Banū 'Abd-ul-Qais and Muṣ'ab b. Zubair to the people of Medina For this job, the Holy Prophet had not entrusted them any work pertaining to open caliphate. Their responsibility was to call people towards Islam and impart to them the teachings of the Qur'ān and the Tradition. Many rules, which are often framed for the missionaries to be sent abroad to serve the cause of the secret caliphate, have been more or less taken from the policy and practice adopted by the Holy Prophet.

After the death of Shāh Walīyullāh, his eldest son Shāh 'Abd-ul-'Azīz, entitled as Shams-ul-Hind, intensified the movement started by his father. The membership of the movement increased and the number of selfless workers also went up. This movement did not end there completely, and continued until the year

1339/1920 when apparently it came to an end with the death of Shaikh-ul-Hind, Maulānā Maḥmūd-ul-Ḥasan of Deobund.[23]

In the year 1383/1963 "Shāh Walīyullāh Academy" had been officially established with its head office at Hyderabad by the Auqaf Department of the West Pakistan Government.[24]

Shāh Ṣāḥib's Aims and Aspirations. What Shāh Walīyullāh wanted to see it achieved, what were his aims and aspirations, and for what was he so anxious and impatient? All this is contained in the following verse of the Qur'ān:

> "It is He Who has sent His Apostle with guidance and the religion of truth, to proclaim it over all religions even though the polytheists like it not."[25]

Commenting on this verse he argues that even though the fall of the empires of Chosroes and Caesar was equivalent to the complete prevalence of Islam as achieved during the reign of the first two Caliphs, this is not permissible for the Muslims that they should remain content with their present deplorable condition with the sweet memory of their glorious past.

He says that the prevalence of Islam should continue uninterruptedly, and be of such a nature that the rest of the world should stand before it in sub-

23. Maulānā 'Ubaidullāh Sindhī, *Shāh Walīyullāh or Un ki Siyāsi Taḥrik*, pp. 143-46.

24. This Academy is the outcome of a trust made by Sayyid 'Abd-ur-Raḥīm Shāh's wife of Sujāwal, solely for the propagation of the teachings and philosophy of Shāh Walīyullāh.

25. Sūrah al-Barā'at, verse 33.

mission. Islam should be perpetually predominant, magnificent, illustrious and splendidly clear. Its arguments and proofs must be convincing and unequivocal, demonstrating its superiority and excellence.[26]

He, however, suggests some ways of proclaiming the prevalence of one religion over other religions, and says that it is the duty of the ruling caliph (ruler) to take note of them. For example, he should make a public demonstration of the customs and practices of his religion, because religious practices and rites are an open truth by which a follower of one religion is distinguished from that of the other. A Muslim stands out recognised from others by his own practices, namely, circumcision, veneration of the mosques, announcement of the prayer-call and offering prayers with congregation, etc. It is also the duty of the ruler to prevent Muslims from openly adopting the customs and systems of other religions, and to take strong measures to make them follow the *Sharī'ah* and should not give them any freedom to treat it in any way they like. Apart from that, he should bear in mind that as the prevalence achieved through the use of sword cannot completely conquer the minds of the people, he should, therefore, try to convince them through press and platform with arguments and proofs, that Islam is the best, the simplest, the most clear in its limits and is the most beneficial for both the common and the special. Furthermore, it appeals to reason and is a true copy of the life as lived by the prophets. He should try to

26. *Izālat-ul-Khafā'*, Vol. I, p. 46.

show to them that religions other than Islam were either not transmitted by the infallible ones or that some of their injunctions were in clash with the basic principles of religion, or that many a change had come in them; as such, obedience to them could not be considered admissible.[27]

The above-mentioned method as suggested by Shāh Ṣāḥib for gaining the prevalence of Islam is practicable and can prove useful in the context of the present times. It is, therefore, necessary for every Islamic State wherever it be to follow and act according to the principles of Islam properly. The religious signs must be adequately demonstrated, and publicly exhibited. Missionary activities should be intensified, for which sincere and zealous workers should be prepared, and then scattered throughout the world to prove to the people both through tradition and reason the superiority of Islam.

Jihād *and Pan-Islamism*. Besides what Shāh Ṣāḥib feels so sorry about and for which he so bitterly laments is the apathy and negligence on the part of the Muslims towards *Jihād* which in fact is continuous and permanent. So long as the spirit of *Jihād* was alive among them, they were made successful and victorious wherever they went, but no sooner it disappeared from them than they were subjugated and held in contempt everywhere. The verse of the Holy Qur'ān: "And fight on with them until there is no more tumult or oppression, and there prevail justice and faith in God al-

27. *Ḥujjatullāh*, Vol. I, pp. 119; 192; Vol. II, p. 197; *al-Budūr-ul-Bāzighah*, pp. 189-92.

together and everywhere, but if they cease, verily God does see all that they do,"[28] clearly points out the necessity of the continuation of *Jihād* until the emergence of Islam as a dominant force.[29]

In the existing times, it is the duty of the Muslim States to revive the spirit of *Jihād* and be always ready for sacrifice. It is, however, possible and is quite likely that the world conditions slowly and gradually may so shape themselves as to enable them to meet at one and the same platform, and co-operate with each other as far as practicable, whether through the formation of a commonwealth or some other organisation. The noble purpose, namely, the achievement of the domination of Islam, can be fulfilled only when the Muslims make an all-round progress. Such a progress is again possible only when the Muslim nations throughout the world sink their differences, come closer together and work unitedly. The idea of pan-Islamism conceived by Shāh Walīyullāh appears to be difficult to materialise these days, as nationalism is dominating religion, but to aspire and work for the establishment of Islam as the greatest international force and power is indeed one of the principal articles of faith.

28. Sūrah al-Anfāl, verse 39.

29. *Ḥujjatullāh*, Vol. II, p. 173 :

و غلبة الدين على سائر الاديان لا يتحقق الا بالجهاد ـ ـ ـ فاذا تركوا الجهاد و اتبعوا أذناب البقر احاط بهم الذل و غلب عليهم أهل سائر الاديان۔

Izālal-ul-Khafā', Vol. I, p. 283:

بعثت آنحضرت صلعم بشريعت غرا نعمت عظيم و لطف جسيم است و قتال بنی آدم که لذاته قبيح بود برائی همين مصلحت تجويز کرده شد ـ

Every person, as is well known, bears love for his country. The Egyptians and the Pakistanis, in spite of belonging to the same faith, are separately maintaining their national entity, Neither of them would tolerate the rule of the other. Now, if any international Islamic organisation is formed, the participation of all the Muslim States therein would be on the equal footing. Every country would remain independent in itself, and their getting together and co-operating with each other would form some sort of an international Islamic organisation.[30]

International Revolution. Maulānā 'Ubaidullāh Sindhī, while shedding light upon the verse: "It is He Who sent His Apostle with guidance. . ." explains as under:

"This verse publicly invites people towards an international revolution, and its primary object is to make all people agree on one point. In history we see that a certain community professes a certain religion, and then subsequently that religion becomes the sacred part of its national life. In like manner, there came into existence a separate religion for every community. But the Qur'ān presents to the world one religion for all, and its sole aim is to make that religion prevail upon all other religions. There are, however, only two ways for achieving this prevalence. One way is to make it dominate other religions through preaching and exhortation; but had this way been possible, there would not have been any necessity for taking up arms and waging wars, and all the people would have accepted this religion of their own accord; but the words at the end of the verse, 'Even though the polytheists like it not' do signify that it would be to the dislike of the polytheists to see Islam dominating. The verse clearly points out the fact that their

30. Professor Muḥammad Sarwar, *Maulānā 'Ubaidullāh Sindhī, Ḥālāt-i-Zindagi, Ta'limāt aur Siyāsi Afkār*, pp. 24, 236-37.

dislike would certainly come in the way of Islam. The other way is the creation of a most powerful centre which could make Islam prevail through the use of force. It is being given out these days that domination should be achieved through peaceful methods; in other words, there is no need to fight and bring about a revolution: but it must be remembered that the nature of man is such that it is not always possible to put up with it peacefully, and sometimes one is compelled to the use of force."[31]

During the reign of the Orthodox Caliphs (*Khulafā'-i-Rāshidīn*), Islam most probably spread through the sword and the use of force and not through the force of argument or by reconciliation.[32]

In the end we would like to give a summary of the piteous appeal he had made to almost all the classes of people of his time, who had become corrupt from every point of view.

"I tell the rulers that this time, it is the will of God that you should draw out your swords from the scabbards, and should not insert them back until God makes a distinction between the Muslims and the infidels, and frees the weak and helpless from their hands. You continue your fight against the infidels and the idolaters, until the religion of God prevails. Furthermore, it is the desire of God that you should appoint a just governor (*amīr*) in every part of the country, at a distance of three to four days' journey from here [Delhi], and make such arrangement that everything is done according to the Law (*Sharī'ah*).

"I ask the governors (*amīrs*). Why don't you fear God? You are so engrossed in the fleeting pleasures of life that you have completely forgotten your subjects, with the result that some of them are devouring the others. Is it not a fact that you

31. *Shāh Waliyullāh aur Un kā Falsafah*, pp. 158-61.
32. *Al-Qaul-ul-Jamīl*:

و ان دخول الناس فى الاسلام فى ايامهم (أيام الخلفاء) كان غالبا بالقهر و السيف لا بالتأليف و اظهار البرهان و لا طوعا و لا رغبة .

drink wine publicly? Have you not set up dens for gambling and debauchery? Is it not a fact that in such a vast country like this, the penal laws (*Ḥudūd-i-Sharī·ah*) are not being enforced for the last seven centuries ? The weak one is greedily swallowed, and the strong is left untouched. Your minds are lost in delicious dishes of food, beautiful women, splendid garments and stately buildings. You do not raise your heads in submission to God at any time, but remember Him only with lips during your (idle) talk, as if by so doing, there will come a revolution in the world, and you say that God is All-Powerful, He will bring the revolution Himself, but remember revolution never comes this way. . . .

"I tell the soldiers : O soldiers, God has raised you for the Holy War, and for the purpose of making the truth prevail, and that you subdue the idolaters and root out their idolatry, but you have neglected this all, and are anxiously applied to the increase of wealth. You drink wine, injure and harm the people. Have fear of God, be firm and patient in your fight with the enemies and follow the path of the *Sharī'ah* very strictly." [33]

At another place Imām Walīyullāh has given expression to the following words which need to be seriously considered :

"I am a stranger amongst you: you do not recognise me properly. There is a crown on my head, and a sword in my hand. My heart is gentle and kind, my tongue is very sweet. O people, return to God, live in peace, keep no ill-will and do not separate. Remember, whosoever will be hostile to me (and turn away from my teachings) will certainly be the loser." [34]

33. *Tafhimāt*, Vol. I, pp. 215-17. (Revolution, particularly social, always comes after many a sacrifice and bloodshed.)

34. Ibid., Vol. II, p. 53.

Chapter VIII

THE SOCIO-ECONOMICS

HUMAN being during his span of life in this world comes across many difficulties. Wise persons have found out the solution of some of these difficulties and are still busy in finding out the solution of the others. The ways and means by which, with little trouble and in short time, one can tide over his social and economic difficulties, are called *Irtifāqāt* In other words, *Irtifāq* means a work done collectively and with co-operation. The word *Irtifāq* is derived from *Rifq* which means gentleness or the use of gentleness. It means that, though the beneficial things abound in the world, they do not come to man for his use of their own accord, but he has to approach them with gentleness.[1]

Man's *Irtifāq* has four stages.

The First Stage (*the Jungle Life*) In this stage, every individual being stands in need of a few basic necessities of life: the food for the satisfaction of hunger, the clothes for the protection against heat and cold, and the shelter to safeguard his life The fulfilment of these three necessities is the very requirement of his nature, and he knows them instinctively. Accordingly, he discovers one or the other method of

1. *Al-Budūr-ul-Bāzighah*, p. 65 ; 'Ubaidullāh Sindhī, *Ilhām-ur-Raḥmān*, p. 26.

cultivation and digs a well for the supply of water, and prepares some partially cooked food to satisfy his hunger. Later on, he begins to tame some animals and prepares from their skin a covering for his body; and in order to safeguard himself from the attack of the enemies, he builds a house of straw and reeds. Besides, he keeps a woman with himself, legally or illegally, to satisfy his sexual urge and desires that nobody should interfere with him in his connection with her. An example of the first *Irtifāq* is discernible in the life of Adam.[2]

In the beginning, man was instinctively directed towards these necessary requirements. If they had not been made available to him, he could not have survived. He received this guidance as the bees receive in sucking the particular kinds of flowers, preparing honey, building the honeycomb, living together in peace and following their queen. In short, there is a separate law for every species of animals. These peculiarities, namely, the search for food, clothing, shelter and lifemate are, however, common to animals and men. But man, according to the requirement of his specific peculiarity, has been given three more specialities which are, however, wanting in animals.[3]

(1) *The Consideration of the General Interests.* The needs of man are not confined to what is merely natural, for he feels within himself the necessity of the far noble and superior things. Mere satisfaction of the

2. *Ḥujjatullāh*, Vol. I, p. 40; *al-Budūr-ul-Bāzighah*, pp. 49, 53-55, 186; *Ta'wil-ul-Aḥādith*, p. 13.

3. *Ḥujjatullāh*, Vol. I, pp. 38-39; *al-Budūr-ul Bāzighah*, pp. 53-55

natural wants like hunger, thirst and sexual urge, etc., does not prepare him for action, but there are some intellectual wants in him as well which encourage him to search for certain gain and avoid certain loss as his reason requires. Accordingly, he always intends to perform actions which not only benefit him, but which lead to the furtherance of the welfare of the people in general. At times, he desires to establish a beneficial social order in a town, and wishes that his character and his self be refined. While looking, to the future and distant gain, he, at times, willingly tolerates the present and immediate loss, and sometimes, taking into consideration the future and distant loss, sacrifices his near and immediate gain. All his endeavour is directed towards the achievement of honour and glory.[4]

(2) *His Love for Beauty and Elegance.* The nature of man, unlike that of the animal is not merely contented with the satisfaction of its needs but he in all his actions, seeks elegance and beauty. As an example, an animal needs food only for the satisfaction of its hunger and for the maintenance of its life, but man even in his food seeks taste and delicacy. He wishes to have fancy dress, a-fine looking house and a beautiful wife.

(3) *The Capability of Invention and Imitation.* Just as the nature of man's needs is different from that of the animal, similarly the nature of inspiration which he receives from God is also different. Unlike the animal, man according to his capabilities receives different kinds of inspirations for his different kinds of

4. *Al-Budūr-ul-Bāzighah*, p. 28.

needs at different times. Taking advantage of those inspirations, he invents useful ways and means for his benefit and welfare. The thought of certain needs does not even occur to certain minds, and to some it does occur, but they do not know the right way of their fulfilment. Someone else receives an inspiration and he discovers a certain useful method which all others learn from him.

In this first stage, in addition to other things, it is also necessary for men to follow someone whom they find more wise and powerful, make him their leader, so that he may help them develop their primary social order, and on certain occasions repulse their enemy from them. It is but natural for them to select someone from among themselves as their guide and then go by his guidance. In the development and growth of society, imitation plays a very important role. Had it not been an inborn quality of man, the society would have taken a very long time for its full development. Man is prepared for imitation, because in respect of reason, there is enough difference among people. Besides, in the search for beauty and elegance, invention of useful schemes, obedience to rules and regulations, and in the freedom to think and meditate, each one differs from the other. This, however, becomes the job of a few select persons, possessing vision and understanding, and who are generous, brave, just and virtuous. They live a life of prosperity and decency and are prepared to work for the development of civilisation. The rest of the people are to follow them. This kind of human stage is considered to be the foundation-stone of man's social life, because no group of persons, however small it be, and removed far away from the villages and and the towns, or living in deserts or on the mountain-tops can be found free from this initial stage of social organisation. In other words, this stage is of such a nature that it is absolutely necessary for people to abide by it for, without so doing, it is not only difficult but impossible for them to lead a social life.[5]

The Second Stage. To examine and test the problems of the first stage on the touchstone of correct experience is the primary principle of the second stage. In the light of experience gathered, every form of such a stage is chosen and adopted in a manner so as to bring maximum possible gain and minimum possible loss If any custom or system is found clashing with that principle, it is to be discarded. Here the ethical values are to be examined afresh. In case they are fair and fine (in the opinion of the perfect and the noble) well and good, otherwise suitable changes are to be brought in them in accordance with the general principle (*Rā'y kullī*). Every aspect of those ethical values should conform to the consideration of the general interest, under which general welfare is given preference over the particular one. For example, when *Rā'y kullī* influences anger, that anger turns out to be an act of bravery. Similarly, when all the sciences (*'ulūm*) come under its influence, they become a piece of philosophy. In like manner, when pride and self-

5. *Ḥujjatullāh*, Vol. I, p. 40.

admiration are refined by the general principle, they are changed into liberality and broadmindedness. In the same manner, if love for women is rectified and corrected by it, that becomes a part of chastity. In this stage, all those manners and proprieties of conduct are discussed which pertain to eating, drinking, association, retirement, dressing, settling and the occasions of pleasure and pain.[6]

For example, it is from the manners of eating and drinking that man should not eat the flesh of a dead animal, nor of that animal whose temperament is far removed from moderation like that of a swine. A man of sound nature will surely dislike it. Apart from that he would first like to wash his hands and mouth and then eat food when it is properly cooked and placed in a vessel; he will use pure water and drink it with a vessel, unlike the animal which puts its mouth into the water. For general cleanliness, it is necessary for him to keep his body well washed, and use toothpick and gargle properly to keep his mouth free from bad odour; shave the hair of his armpit and those below the navel, and trim his beard and the hair of his head in the best possible manner. He should put on good clothes which may cover the larger part of his body and have an extra cover for his private parts as well. Besides, he should also keep his house clean.

Man by nature is inclined to know his future, and this tendency, to a certain extent, is found among all the people of the world. For that, one should avail of

6. Ibid.; *al-Budūr-ul-Bāzighah*, pp. 30-31.

the interpretation of dreams, geomancy and astronomy. It is also necessary that he should try to make his speech eloquent and render his talk clear and understandable. Furthermore, the household administration should be maintained in a better form, and for that the following things should be taken into consideration.

(1) *The Rights and Rules for Husband and Wife.* When man has to perpetuate his progeny, he has to marry and give birth to children, and for that it is necessary that both the husband and the wife should remain in peace and amity. In the breeding of children, the wife's share is by nature greater, and she has the ability to run the family affairs properly and efficiently; and she is by nature more obedient and submissive. The qualities of man are quite different. In reason, understanding and in the knowledge of vocations, he excels woman. He is well versed in doing the hard jobs, has courage to face difficulties, and is by nature inclined to rule. However, they both, despite their individual traits of character, are interdependent for the smooth running of the house administration. As man is by nature jealous and possesses all the passions of manhood, it is necessary that he should have his own lawful wife, otherwise there would be fights and feuds among men. Their marriage ceremony should be performed in public so that anyone else who had an intention of marrying her should give it up for ever It behoves a man that, in addition to dowry, he should spend something more on festivity and rejoicing, so as to win the love of his wife. After marriage it is the duty of both the husband and the wife

to co-operate with each other in making their life prosperous and happy and should equally share the weal and woe. At times, some unpleasant incidents take place which make their further living together impossible. In that case, they should better separate from each other by divorce so as to spend the remainder of their life without worry and fear.

(2) *Upbringing of Children.* They should give good breeding and proper education to their children and take special care of their progress and development. Unusual attention should be paid to their health, and suitable atmosphere be created for the improvement of their character. In return, it is the duty of their children, when they become mature, to take into account those troubles and hardships which their parents had endured for their sake. They must respect and honour them, obey their orders, speak to them gently, be faithful to them and reciprocate what they had done for them.

(3) *Mutual Dealings and the Relations with the Near and Dear.* It is a fact that there are persons in society who are unable to fulfil their needs due to poverty and lack of means. Besides, certain diseases do disable some persons from work. In such adverse conditions, it is the duty of the rich and the well-to-do to help them as far as possible. That is the reason why the wise and prudent persons of the world have considered the extension of sympathy and help to the distressed and the afflicted as a necessary requirement of society. In short, the .ation of the needy and the independent be so fast and thick that each one of them should take

the loss or gain of the other as his own. Such relationship is naturally found among near relatives, and it is due to this reason that at the death of one, the other becomes the heir of his property Mutual help of the relatives at the time of need known in the *Sharī'ah* as *Ṣila'-i-raḥim* is the most important duty.

The first *Irtifāq* is an initial stage in the ladder of man's progress, when the human species had not become ripe as yet. People were living in the jungles and small villages, following their headmen. As time passed the human race which was small in number increased by leaps and bounds. This gave rise to variety in the activities of their lives and substantial increase in their mutual transactions. Their small villages now took the shape of big towns and cities and a good social order came into being, under which they began to spend their lives. This civil life is another name for the second *Irtifāq* and an example of it is found in the life of the Prophet Idrīs (Enoch).[7]

All the four stages of human society follow one another in order. It never happens that the second stage may come before the first. Society sets its foot on every other rung of the ladder after it has placed it on the first one. However, it is not necessary that every second rung of the ladder may not be set foot on until the first one had become complete and perfect from every point of view. What Shāh Ṣāḥib says is that there are certain factors in every stage of society. Some of them happen to be the pillars of that

7. *Ḥujjatullāh*, Vol. I, pp. 40-43 ; *al-Budūr-ul-Bāzighah*, pp. 55-64, 186.

stage without which the next stage of society cannot come into existence; and some factors are such which, if they are wanting, do not affect the existence of that stage of society, save that it would be empty of elegance and fineness. It is, however, possible for the society to reach the next stage even if only the pillars of the preceding one are present there, namely, freedom from natural wants, like food and drink, clothing and shelter. The factors which are to be rendered elegant and fine in the first stage can be produced even after setting foot on the second rung of the ladder. Sometimes, man after having reached the higher stage becomes more capable of bringing perfection, refinement and elegance to the lower stage.[8]

The Third Stage (*Nationalism*). This stage relates to the administration of the big towns and cities in which the mutual relations of different kinds of people living in different towns are to be further improved and established on sound basis. In this *Irtifāq* the whole nation, however large the number of its individuals be, running in lacs and crores, is considered as one single being. Accordingly, if any individual feels some pain somewhere the whole nation feels it, as the whole body feels when a part of it is injured. At this stage, the needs of man go beyond computation, and he wants to excel in all the aspects of life. As it is not possible for him to fulfil all his needs in a better and refined manner singly, he will have to live and co-operate with others in their social life. At this stage, even

8. *Al-Budūr-ul-Bāzighah*, pp. 50-52.

though each one has a separate occupation, their mutual co-operation and help is, however, necessary, which eventually results in the formation of a political order among them. This they badly need at that time. For the maintenance of mutual transactions and dealings, they first need some kind of exchange, which need they fulfil after due consideration by the introduction of gold and siver coins. On account of the multiplicity and diversity of occupations, everyone is busy trying to improve upon his art and profession, and it is here that society becomes fully developed in the proper sense of the word.[9]

Qualifications of a Ruler. In case of an increased population, it is not, however, possible that all the people should always obey the just and fair order and should not go against it. It is, therefore, necessary that there should be a ruler for them, elected by their wise and headmen, who however, should be so able and powerful as to compel them to follow the prescribed law and, thus, check the spread of insecurity and disorder. Such a ruler is expected to possess the following qualifications: He should be a man of good character brave and strong-hearted, otherwise people will dislike him, and the enemies and the mischief-makers will have no fear of him. Besides, he should be tolerant and forbearing and should have the ability to run the country's administration properly. He should be respectable and noble, always anxious for the good and welfare of his subjects. He should know how to

9. *Ḥujjatullāh*, Vol. I, p. 43.

win the hearts of the people, and make himself acceptable among them by his sincerity and the performance of his duty. In other words, as the hunter, in order to hunt his prey, avails of all his guiles and arts, similarly, he should spare no pains in winning the love of his subjects. It is proper for the ruler (the government) to give generous treatment to his subjects, but he should show no remissness in punishing the offenders. However, no hasty step should be taken until the offence of the offender is clearly proved. Those who work in the government selflessly and honestly ought to be given every kind of encouragement. In short, the ruler should be of an enlightened nature, and so experienced and possessed of insight as to undertand the inner self of a man at his very sight, and so far-sighted as to know the result of State affairs before their actual happening.

When the ruler is unable to carry on the administration singly, he surely needs for the various departments of the government a team of efficient and selfless persons who should be very much conscious of their responsibility and the discharge of their duty. At the time of appointment, care should be taken to avoid assigning any post to a person whom, later on, it may be difficult to remove or who may be found unfit or perfidious. The best plan for him at that time is to distribute his work and powers if he is holding the post among two or more persons according to what expediency requires. There are also persons who somehow enter into the government for their selfish ends. They should be brought round somehow to behave properly and be loyal to the government, otherwise they should be compelled to retire. The ruler should not forget that he cannot expect from the servants of his government anything beyond their inborn capacity, as that is impossible.[10]

The heavy work of the government requires large sums of money, for which a treasury is established, the income of which comes from various kinds of taxes. It is the duty of the rich and the wealthy not to avoid the payment of proper taxes, because whatever is collected in the treasury is spent for the good of the common people; and the purpose of the government in establishing it is the welfare of the public and nothing else. But while levying taxes, justice should be shown, and no extraordinary burden be imposed upon the income of the objects. Taxes should be recovered only from those possessing wealth, or from those who own such property which is found increasing every day and who are traders and owners of industries, but even that tax may be levied on them only when their income were to exceed the satisfaction of their necessaries of life.[11]

To guard and preserve the country against the internal as well as the external dangers, the ruler has to organise his army properly, and for that purpose, he has to create conditions under which it may always remain loyal, disciplined and most powerful. The army can be cempletely relied upon only when

10. Ibid., pp. 44-46. 11. Ibid., pp. 46-47.

the government is found doing everything selflessly for the good of its people. Its loyalty corresponds to the popularity the government enjoys amongst its own men. For the luxurious living of the few, the army is not going to ruin itself.

In the third stage (*Irtifāq*) the government has to take in view all the points mentioned above and, in order to keep the society sound and healthy, it has to do the following five things:

(1) Greed, niggardliness and malevolence often give rise to differences among individual beings in society. If they are not suppressed, they will bring in their train fights, murders, loot and plunder. It is, therefore, the duty of the government to arrange for the just settlement of their disputes, and to be so strong and powerful in itself as to be able to remove their differences and enforce its own decisions.

(2) Some people develop bad habits, carry bitter rivalries and come under the pressure of low desires. They should be harassed and threatened to desist from their evil designs, otherwise the existence of the society would be at stake.

(3) There are also individuals in society who are always busy in disrupting the social order. Their intention by that is to lay hands on the properties of others or to seize political power to fulfil their selfish ends. Such mischief-makers and disruptionists do associate with themselves many persons trained in fighting and warfare. It is, therefore, the duty of the government, the party in power, to be always ready

to wage war against them for the preservation and safeguard of the human society and nation.

(4) Thinkers and wise men have always a noble aim and an object before their eyes for the maintenance of the human society in the best possible form, and their intention is that society should work for the achievement of that aim and object. It is, therefore, necessary for the government to endeavour hard towards the attainment of the object they have in view.

(5) Men, on account of their attachment with worldly affairs, generally forget their moral and religious requirements and become negligent. It is, therefore, the duty of the government to make them give up their negligence and make them feel their responsibility towards morality and religion, through advice and admonition. The example of this *Irtifāq* and of the second one is provided in the life of the Prophets Sulaimān (Solomon) and Moses.[13]

The Fourth Stage (*Internationalism*). This is a stage in which mutual relations between various nations take place. When the frontiers of a country are extended far and wide and human population exceeds beyond bounds, the country is divided into various provinces, administered by governors. Every province has its own means of income and its own army to defend it. As all the people are not of the same temperament, and they also differ in their abili-

13. Ibid., p. 47 ; *al-Budūr-ul-Bāzighah*, pp. 72-85 ; *Ta'wil-ul-Aḥadith* p. 50.

ties, there always take place fights and feuds among them leading them to follow the wrong course. They begin to harbour malice and jealousy which incite them to usurp the property of others. When conditions assume that ugly form, people feel the necessity of a very powerful ruler who can safeguard their interests. If he is available and is himself law-abiding, others, less powerful, will, willingly or unwillingly, surrender and obey his order, thus enabling people to live their social life in peace, safety and prosperity.

Duties of a Powerful Ruler. Such a powerful ruler at times finds it but unavoidable to take up arms and fight. In every community there are persons bent upon creating mischief and disorder. They blindly follow their low desires and become the source of disruption in society. They must be compelled to obey the law by the use of force; and those who later on would prove to be a cancer in the body of the community should be ruthlessly persecuted and wiped out. Even after the government is firmly established, events do take place which make it necessary for the ruler to take up the sword in his hand, because the people of bestial nature take to loot and plunder as their profession, and, thus, spread insecurity and disorder everywhere in the country.[14]

As it is known, wars cannot be carried on without necessary provisions. It is, therefore, that the ruler's (government) treasury should remain always full, and he should have so much force at his disposal

14. *Ḥujjatullāh*, Vol. I, pp. 47-48 ; *al-Budūr-ul-Bāzighah*, pp. 85-86.

as to put down mischief, and avail of it at times of emergency. For such a ruler it is necessary to be well informed of the occasions of war and peace. He should so weaken and reduce the force of his enemies as to eliminate the possibility of their future opposition. He should establish an espionage system in the country to keep himself acquainted with the activities of the enemy and then take due precautionary measures in time. The enemy must be so suppressed and subdued as to give the proof of its submissiveness both in words and deeds. Its verbal statements will not be sufficient until and unless they are supported by clear evidences of its sincerity in practice.[15]

Agreement of People on Irtifāqāt. All nations, despite their territorial and religious differences, are agreed upon these *Irtifāqāt* in principle. They acknowledge their soundness and consider it necessary to follow them. All this is the result of the natural requirement of man's specific form.[16]

Let us take it for granted that a man is born in some barren land and, as such, is deprived of formal education but, in spite of that, he needs to satisfy his hunger, thirst and sexual urge; besides, he will need some shelter to save himself from heat, cold and rain. Sexual urge, however, will compel him to keep some legal or illegal matrimonial connection with some woman, which will bring in its wake the birth of children, whose number will multiply by the passage

15. *Ḥujjatullāh*, Vol. I, p. 48; *al-Budūr-ul-Bāzighah*, pp. 85-87.
16. *Al-Budūr-ul-Bāzighah*, p. 94.

of time. From family and tribe, it will take the shape of a large community and nation. The increase in population will surely give rise to various kinds of their connections and then their maintenance, and this is how a society comes into being and is gradually developed.[17]

In short the four stages in the life of man are as follows:

(1) The jungle life, when the society was too small living in huts and hamlets.
(2) The life of towns and cities when the society appreciably developed.
(3) When the society assumed the form of a nation with a very large population.
(4) And when the society, having made developments all round, took the shape of an international organisation.[18]

Causes of Corruption. The above institutions, which came to be established for the fulfilment of the needs of man, become corrupt and obsolete with the passage of time. Many kinds of evils creep in, rendering them useless and harmful. The main reason for their corruption is that the leadership of people goes into the hands of those who ignore the absolute good and the consideration of general interests which are required for the welfare of the masses, and take to the satisfaction of their low desires. Majority happens to follow them with the result that the foundation of civilisation and culture becomes badly shaken. To

17. Ibid., p. 49. 18. Ibid., p. 51.

save the society from extinction, Nature on such occasions brings into existence certain persons who root out that corruption and reform the society afresh. Shāh Sāhib has, however, made this matter very clear at many places, that the moral and ethical side of man's life is largely dependent upon his economic conditions, as he says: "The social virtues of men are completely destroyed at a time when they are forced to live under hard and difficult financial stringencies; and it is only for the sake of bread that they are made to work like beasts of burden. When mankind is faced with such a calamity, God paves the way to save it. Accordingly, He inspires one of His chosen ones to rise and do the needful. The destruction of the Pharaoh, Caesar and Chosroes was the result of that inspiration."[19]

Imām Walīyullāh, as has already been mentioned, does not fear or hesitate in telling the truth, and has been exposing the misdeeds of the government of his times. Referring to their luxurious living and the absence of moral values, he says: "When the Persian and Roman Empires continued for long, the rulers and the high-ups lost themselves in the ease and comfort of life, and completely forgot the Hereafter. Their luxurious living went to such an extent that if any chief did not have a crown worth lakhs of dīnārs to wear on his head, people used to find fault with him. You see the prevailing conditions of your

19. Ibid., p. 53; *Ḥujjatullāh*, Vol. I, p. 106.

country which are in no way better than theirs."[20]

It is clear that these provisions of comfort and luxury cannot be available without spending large sums of money. In consequence, heavy and intolerable taxes were being levied upon the labour class, the peasantry, the business community and the craftsmen, for the payment of which they (the labour class in particular) worked like animals day and night, and, as such, the helpless and the poor have had no time to remember God and the Hereafter. The hungry and the uncovered is neither of this world nor of the Hereafter [21]

Apart from the luxurious living of the high, and the imposition of heavy and burdensome taxes, the other cause of the break-up of society is that some persons like sepoys and the *'Ulamā'* (scholars) who consider themselves entitled to government stipends do not work at all, and, thus, become an unwholesome burden upon the State exchequer. Giving of gifts and grants to the ascetics and the poets has also become a habit of the rulers now-a-days. Society's well-being lies in the lightening of the taxes and the employment of civil and military staff according to requirement.[22]

Proper Distribution of Labour. Besides, some people follow the professions they are not fit for, and this in turn cuts at the very root of social development. There is a man who is very hungry but un-

20. *Ḥujjatullāh*, Vol. I, pp, 105-06 ; Vol. II. p. 132.
21. Ibid., Vol. I, pp. 105-06.
22. Ibid., p. 54.

fortunately he takes a profession which does not satisfy his hunger. Naturally, he perforce will be inclined to beggary and other low and hateful practices. Again, there are people who, in spite of being robust and strong, do not work hard and rush into indecent occupations.[23]

The other strong reason for the decomposition of society is that, if there is a population of ten thousand, the majority does not busy itself in the increase of production, with the result that the population starves. As such, there is a need for the proper distribution of labour. Similarly, if the majority indulges in luxurious living, it will become a burden on the nation and a contagion which will go on infecting slowly and gradually the whole population, eventually reducing it to a state of one being bitten by a rabid dog.[24]

Economic Conditions Influence Man's Character. However, Imām Walīyullāh cites one more fact in particular, that the society corrupts and disintegrates when some people take to exploitation and monopolisation. They attempt at seizing the properties of others, and, thus, all the avenues of their income and livelihood are closed. Social economy has a greater impact upon the character of man. It is, therefore, necessary that for the maintenance of character and moral values, a just economic order (proper distribution of wealth) be established in human society. Until and unless this kind of order is established, the

23. *Al-Budūr-ul-Bāzighah*, pp. 53-65.
24. *Ḥujjatullāh*, Vol. II, pp. 105-06.

beauty of social character will never appear. One aspect of life invariably affects the other, as all of them are closely connected. And it is indeed these economic conditions which determine man's character.[25]

Human society, according to Shāh Walīyullāh, can never become completely perfect, but it can come near to perfection. Individual beings are like the limbs of a body and as Zaid, for example, can never be perfect in his health from every point of view, for there will certainly be some imbalance and want of equilibrium somewhere in his body, similarly is the case of a human society which can never be in a state of balanced health.[26]

He is, however, of opinion that the knowledge of the natural requirements of men can give a correct lead in the fixation of aims and objects of a society. It should then be its sole purpose to fulfil them and make provision to meet men's primary needs, such as bread for the belly, covering for the body and house for the dwelling.

Bearing all these facts in mind, Imām Walīyullāh has laid much emphasis upon the improvement of the economic condiitions of men and for that has advised that everybody should do something with his

25. Ibid., Vol. II, p. 125; *al-Budūr-ul-Bāzighah*, p. 51:

انما الاخلاق بالاحوال لا بالعلوم -

26. *Al-Budūr-ul-Bāzighah*, pp. 48-49:

و افراد الانسان كالاعضاء للعناية الازلية المنعقدة فى صورة نوع الانسان فاذا صلحت الاعضاء كلها بالفرض فهو الصحة التامة والاعتدال الحقيقى و هو كالممتنع - - -

own hands to earn, so that he may not be a burden on the government and the people.[27]

His appeal to people in general: "O children of Adam! whosever from you has bread to eat, water to drink, shelter to dwell in, clothes to cover the body and in addition to these all has a wife also, then he is given everything in the world. It now behoves him to remain content, and follow the course of moderation in his living."[28]

These are the basic needs of man; if these are fulfilled, he gets almost all the things of the world. In support of this he gives a quotation from the Tradition of the Holy Prophet: "Man has no right save of three things: a house to dwell in, clothes to cover his body, and bread and water for his belly."[29]

Shāh Walīyullāh takes the meaning of the word *'Afw* in the Holy Qur'ān to be that which exceeds the necessary needs of life. By restricting needs to "necessary" he has indeed suggested a very useful solution of the economic problems.[30]

Divine Wisdom requires, he says, that human society should not lag behind the second and third stages of social development (*Irtifāq*). This is the reason why no prophet has ever asked his people to abandon society and go to stay in jungles and on mountain-tops, as it is against the very interests

27. *Tafhīmāt*, Vol. I, p. 218:

ولا تکونوا کلا علی الناس و علی الخلفاء ۔

28. Ibid., Vol. I, p. 218.

29. *Ḥujjatullāh*, Vol. II, p. 85.

30. *Fatḥ-ur-Raḥmān*, Sūrah al-Baqarah, verse 219.

of man himself [31]

Apart from that, the character of man does not come to light and is not known but only when there is a clash with the people. Without contact and without any association with different kinds of people and varying social orders, the beauty of man's character does not become clear.[32]

At times, some persons leaving the primary things of the first stage half-done begin to give more attention to those of the second one with the result that society does not become stable. Man's good lies in this that when the fourth stage were to go out of his hands, he should hold fast to the third one. Similarly, if he were to lose the third one, he should stick to the second one and so on. But because people have no adequate knowledge of the different stages of social development (*Irtifāq*), so they stick to the stage they are acquainted with, with the result that society degenerates, and the whole social structure starts cracking [33]

It is the responsibility of the people living in populated cities to remain in amity and friendship with each other. Every phase as a whole must see that the prop of everything in them is raised on friendship and affection.[34]

31. *Al-Budūr-ul-Bāzighah*, p. 190.
32. *Ḥujjatullāh*, Vol. I, p. 51 :
والاخلاق لا تظهر الا عند مزاحمات من بنى النوع -
33. *Al-Budūr-ul-Bāzighah*, pp. 89-90.
34. Ibid., p. 52. Iqbal :
ہیں جذب باھمی سے قائم نظام سارے پوشیدہ ہے یہ نکتہ تاروں کی زندگی میں

Necessity of Revolution. Shāh Walīyullāh was a revolutionary. It is, therefore, that he has encouraged people to work for it if the circumstances were so to necessitate. This is, however, clear from what follows.

When society (government) grows corrupt beyond proportion, it becomes necessary to bring about a revolution. A social institution under which the people are deprived of their primary needs of life is like an abscess in the body which the sooner it is removed the better it would be. The persons who know wherein lies the general welfare feel it at that time as their bounden duty to bring about revolution. But it should be borne in mind that the bringing about of a revolution is a very distressful and hard job, as, in addition to the sacrifice of life and property, one has at times to part even with one's beloved country. Such sacrifices can be made by those who are very sincere, self-confident and have the ability and courage to face the situations, however serious, with patience and endurance. For the working of such a revolution, sometimes, one has to struggle through protests, at times through demonstrations, and at times through raising of slogans, etc., and on certain occasions one has to put up an actual fight. Whatever sacrifice is made in this direction is reckoned from the best of actions.[35]

Islam Must Prevail. Islam has come to establish

35. *Ḥujjatullāh*, Vol. I, pp. 49-50; Vol. II, pp. 170-71;
والمدن الفاسدة التی یغلب علیها نفوس سبعیة و یکون لهم تمنع
شدید انما هو بمنزلة الآکلة فی بدن الانسان لا یصح الانسان الا بقلعه -

the fourth stage of social development, namely, to become the greatest international power in the world, which could stand the challenge of time. It is, therefore, the sacred duty of all the Muslims throughout the world to work hard and spare no pains for the establishment of an international Islamic organisation which could successfully face the combined opposition. "The completion of favour" (*wa atmamtu 'alaikum ni'matī*) takes practical shape only when such a greatest power is created.[36]

It, however, cannot be denied that under the conditions prevailing today the formation of an international organisation seems to be difficult, but the Muslims must always have that aim in view and avail of every opportunity and situation to transform that idea of pan-Islamism as conceived by Shāh Walīyullāh into dead reality. This object can certainly be achieved if Muslim countries come closer to each other, sink their differences and work together as a single unit on international basis as far as possible. Until the international government of the Muslims comes into being, it is necessary for them to work zealously and enthusiastically for the stability and fortification of their national governments (the third *Irtifāq*). Every nation should make itself strong from religious, moral and political point of view. They should always remain vigilant, ready and well prepared for fight, keep themselves adequately informed of the latest developments in the modern methods of warfare, and infuse the

36. Ibid., Vol. I, p. 47.

spirit of *Jihād* into the hearts of their people.[37]

Unfortunately, no proper attention in these days is being paid to the teachings of the Holy Qur'ān with regard to the making of this worldly life strong and successful by taking advantage of all the possible means. Self-defence and necessary preparations against a possible attack of an enemy and making life prosperous and strong is one of the duties Islam has enjoined on the Muslims. For example, there come these words in the Holy Qur'ān: "Against them make ready your strength to the utmost of your power, including steeds of war, to strike terror into (the hearts of) the enemies of God and your enemies."[38] At another place God says: "If they had intended to come out, they would certainly have made some preparation therefor."[39] Again, there is a verse: "The unbelievers wish you were negligent of your arms and your baggage, to assault you in a single rush."[40]

According to a Tradition, the defence of Muslims is better and more rewarding than the supererogatory prayers and fasts; and one day's patrolling of the frontiers is better than one month's prayers and

37. *Al-Budūr-ul-Bāzighah*, pp. 192, 198-99:

وكن من الجاهرين بانحصار الغرض الا لاهى من قبل الانسانية فى شيوع هذه الملة و ظهورها تارة على وطيرة الارتفاق الثالث و تارة على وطيرة الارتفاق الرابع ـ ـ ـ ومن مقاصد شرع رسول الله صلعم ابراز الدين الحنيفى و اظهاره على وطيرة الارتفاق الرابع بأن لا يوجد على وجه الارض احد الا و قد غلبه الدين الحنيفى بحيث لا يمكن له مقاومته ـ ـ ـ

38. Sūrah Anfāl, verse 60. 39. Sūrah Taubah, verse 46.
40. Sūrah Nisā', verse 102.

fasting.

At present, the world is not devoid of the third stage of social development (national government), and if it is ever deprived of it, that would be a catastrophe.[41]

The fact to which Shāh Walīyullāh draws our attention is that since the religion of Islam has come for the establishment of the greatest international power and when its domination is to continue for ever, it can be rightly insured only when the Muslim nations make themselves strong both morally and materially, draw closer and work together as far as possible. It is high time the Muslims realise the importance and necessity of unity, forget their past jealousies and work for the solidarity of Islam and lose no time and effort to make themselves the greatest power in the world.[42]

41. *Al-Budūr-ul-Bāzighah*, p 95.

42. Ibid., p, 199:

و لما كان هذا الاظهار مثل تسلط اسكندر بالارتفاق الرابع و يزيد عليه بأنه يقصد به ابقاء الدين على وجهه طول الزمان وادامة التسلط غضا طريا وجب من هذا السبيل آمور، منها ابطال الملل و اعدامها و الزجر عن الخوض، و منها ايجاب التمذهب بهذا المذهب -

Ḥujjatullāh, Vol. II, p. 197:

- - أن احدى المصالح التى بعث النبى صلعم لها التنويه بالملة الاسلامية وجعلها أعلى الملل و أعظمها لا يتحقق الا بأن يكون لهم طول على من سواهم -

Chapter IX

LIFE AFTER DEATH

TO understand the reality of the other world, it is necessary to know the soul first. The commentators in general have included the problem of soul in allegorical ones with the result that no thinker dares approach this problem. In the opinion of Shāh Walīyullāh, life after death, which the Holy Qur'ān describes, is within the reach of human intellect. He has made this matter clear in the very introduction of his *Ḥujjatullāh-ul-Bālighah* that the realities of the future life, like the questioning in the grave, the weighing of the actions, the crossing of the Bridge and the seeing of God, are intellectually comprehensible.[1]

But it may be remembered that, according to Shāh Ṣāhib, the intellect which is generally understood as having its connection with the mind (*nafs*) is not correct. He, on the contrary, is of opinion that it is connected with the perceptive (*Idrākiyyah*) faculty which is an agent of the mind in the world of space, and is the nearest of the bodies (*Jismāniyyah*) towards it. The proof of this, he says, is that the intellect in

1. *Alṭāf-ul-Quds* (with Urdu translation), pp. 98-99; *Ḥujjatullāh*, "*Muqaddimah*," p. 9:

فمن هذا القسم سؤال القبر و وزن الاعمال و المرور على الصراط و الرؤية - - - ولكن ضاق نطاق المعقول عنها - - - ونحن نقول آمنا بذالک كله على بينة من ربنا و شهد له المعقول عندنا ـ

this sense, namely, in the sense of its having connection with the mind faculty sometimes goes wrong, while, as a matter of fact, no non-material ever goes wrong.[2]

Nasmah. There exists a subtle vapour in the body of man, which is the creation of the essence of his four humours. Those four humours are: blood, phlegm, yellow bile and black bile, but among them the proportion of blood is large, so much so that it can be said that the subtle vapour is its essence. These four humours are made of four elements, namely, air, earth, water and fire. This vapour is just like a white fog, pervading the whole body and is responsible for its functioning.

Physicians know very well that so long as it is in the body, man is alive, but as soon as it separates from it, he is dead. We call this subtle vapour *Nasmah* (the spirit). It is in the body, as the rose-water is in the rose, or as the fire is in the charcoal, but this spirit is of inferior type.[3]

It is one of the qualities of this *Nasmah* hat it can taste without a tongue and can hear without the use of ears. This is so because the common sense (*al-ḥiss-ul-mushtarik*) is always present in it (in *Nasmah*), by means of which every sense-faculty aided by the intellectual one can have the perception of things prior to their happening. For example, it is from the sense of tasting that when a man sees some delicious eatable, his mouth, without having tasted it, becomes watery

2. *Al-Khair-ul-Kathir*, p. 53.

3. *Ḥujjatullāh*, Vol. I, pp 18-19; *Fuyūḍ-ul-Ḥaramain*, Mashhad,

merely at the sight of it.[4]

When man dies, either of serious illness or of a deadly blow, his *Nasmah* goes very weak, because the four humours responsible for its creation are no more there, but it does not completely disappear. Providence then comes to its help, with the result that its life gains strength, and it becomes able to see, hear and speak. As the body was a steed for the *Nasmah* in this world, similarly the *Nasmah* would serve as a steed for the real soul (*al-Rūḥ-ul-Ḥaqīqī*) in the world to come.[5]

By the real soul is meant the human soul which the philosophers call "the Rational Soul" (*Nāfs Nāṭiqah*). Contrary to the *Nasmah* which goes on changing in quality and quantity from the very birth of a man until his death, the soul undergoes no change whatsoever. It is directly connected with the *Nasmah* and through it with the rest of the body.

As the Rational Soul is extremely refined and subtle, it can have connection only with a matter of similar quality. That matter should be so moderate and temperate as to bear the maximum possible resemblance to the soul, so that it (soul) could manifest itself therein adequately. *Nasmah* is extremely subtle and is in a state of equilibrium ; as such, it is quite fit for relationship with it.

4. *Al-Budūr-ul-Bāzighah*, pp. 33-34; *Fuyūḍ-ul-Ḥaramain*, Mashhad, 2.
5. *Ḥujjatullāh*, Vol. I, p. 19 :

و قد تحقق عندنا بالوجدان الصحيح ان الموت انفکاک النسمة عن البدن لفقد استعداد البدن لتوليدها لا انفکاک الروح القدس عن النسمة - - -

Death. At the time of death, it is the *Nasmah* which separates from the body and its separation becomes the cause of death. The connection of soul, however, remains with it intact. It is absolutely wrong to believe that the soul separates from the *Nasmah*. The soul penetrates the *Nasmah* there as it had penetrated the body here, and as the body was a vehicle for it in this world, similarly the *Nasmah* would be the vehicle for the soul in the next world. In other words, the *Nasmah* would be the body of the soul.[6]

When man dies, his earthly body decays, but its decay in no way affects the soul, as it maintains its connection with the *Nasmah* which does not completely disintegrate; and its (*Nasmah's*) condition at that time is like that of an expert writer with his fingers cut off, still retaining the faculty of writing. If the *Nasmah* were to disintegrate, the soul bereft of it is not capable of any reward or liable to any punishment. It can be rewarded or punished only when attached to the matter. As, for example, the body of man after his death neither gets fever nor develops any abscess, nor does it feel any pain, similarly God does not deal with anything in a manner which is radically opposed to the requirement of its nature. It is, however, the natural requirement of the soul that it should have the same connection with its matter as an animal or human form has with its body. The *Nasmah* after man's death retains in its airy essence almost all the

6. Ibid., pp 32-33; *al-Budūr-ul-Bāzighah*, pp. 32-34; *Tafhīmāt*, Vol. I, p. 171.

faculties of the head and heart.[7]

Stage of Grave. Man after his death is transported to a world which is named by the prophets "the world of grave" (*'Ālam-ul-Qabr*), an explanation of which is, however, necessary.

Man dreams in sleep, and all that he sees there is the reflection of his thoughts and knowledge. When he was awake, those thoughts and knowledge were in a state of suppression on account of his various occupations. But in sleep, when the sense faculties stop functioning, they freely make their appearance. For example, a man of bilious nature sees in his dream that he is in a dry jungle and it is the summer season, and a hot wind is blowing. Then all of a sudden that jungle catches fire. He tries his best to get out of it somehow but cannot find a way of escape. By that time the fire destroying the jungle envelops him and he on that account feels intense pain. Now if a man were to think a little, he will find that those were exactly his own thoughts which had appeared to him in his sleep in a particular form. In short, the world of grave should be taken like this world of dreams. The only difference is that from the world of dreams man wakes up very soon, but in the world of grave he will have that deep sleep from which he cannot rise before the Day of Judgment. If a man were not to wake up from his sleep here, he will surely take that dream and what he sees therein to be a reality and an actual happening. The following example will help to under-

7. *Tafhimāt*, Vol. I, pp. 166-67.

stand the stage of grave better. A man overcome by fierceness and cruelty in this world will see in the grave a wild beast like a lion or a wolf scratching him with its claws. The miser will see a serpent or a scorpion biting or stinging him. The revelation of the Celestial Sciences will appear to him in the form of two angels, who will ask him about his Creator, his religion and the Prophet Muḥammad. If the actions of man are good and fair, he will see angels with beautiful faces, carrying silken clothes and musk in their hands. A door of Paradise would be opened for him, and he would be called by a fair name from all sides; but if he happens to be an unbeliever, he will see angels with fiery eyes and black faces carrying hammers in their hands.[8]

All these occurrences are the facts, and there is no metaphor in them, nor is there any comparison of the non-material things with the material ones. It is their customary explanation. And there are two ways by which such occurrences can be explained. One way is common and known to all, namely, that in which the occurrence is stated as it is. For example, in case of illness it is said that so and so is suffering from fever or headache. The other way is that of a physician who would rather say that biliousness has prevailed upon him and he, therefore, has this fever or headache. But prophets always employ the first way, the known type of expression, namely, the one spoken and understood by the common people.[9]

8. *Ḥujjatullāh*, Vol. I, pp. 34-36.
9. *Al-Budūr-ul-Bāzighah*, pp. 149-52.

Man, however, will have twofold pain or pleasure in the grave. One is the apprehension of the good or bad actions, and the other is that some angels will be inspired to appear to him in some beautiful or in some ugly and awful form, thus becoming the cause of his pleasure or pain.[10]

If he is not beguiled by the charms of this world, he will not feel any pain at the time of his departure from it. This is quite clear. A man intending to go on a pilgrimage, or on some distant journey, naturally takes stock of all the rigours and hardships he has to come across; despite that he leaves and does not feel any distress or difficulty in his way. The departure from the ease and comfort of his home, from his property and from his family and children does not give him any trouble. Another man, engrossed in the luxuries of life, with an extraordinary attachment to his family, children and property, if he leaves for a distant journey, is certainly troubled at his separation from all these things with the result that he makes very slow progress in his journey and feels it as a heavy load at every step. In short, the pain or pleasure which man will have in the grave is the result of his own actions. It is his actions which assume suitable forms there, and become the cause of his agony or joyfulness.[11]

The actions of the animals, even though optional, leave no abiding impression on their hearts. It is

10. *Ḥujjatullāh*, Vol. I, p. 36; *Tafhimāt*, Vol. I, pp. 252-53.
11. *Al-Budūr-ul-Bāzighah*, pp. 150-51.

temporary and disappears very soon. The case of man is quite different. Whatever action he performs, if done deliberately, its impression stays on his heart and the heart, in a way, absorbs that impression and makes it as its own. The intention for action, however, first proceeds from his Rational Soul and, after the action is performed, returns to it rather comparatively strong and clings to it and becomes inseparable. Thus, his actions done with the full presence of his mind are preserved in his *Nasmah* and after death, when his body will decompose, they will appear to him in true colours.

When sufficient time passes as to the stay of man in the grave, his "Nasmic" constitution will get disrupted, and he will ultimately rise from his deep sleep. The Rational Soul will, however, remain independent as ever, and the *Nasmah* as a whole will follow it unreservedly. The reason of this change is that the supply of food which the *Nasmah* used to receive for its maintenance stopped since long, and, during that period, many changes took place which demanded the disintegration of every elemental object.

Judgment Day. On the Judgment Day the individual peculiarities of men brought about by the combination of elements will, however, vanish. Every self will appear reflecting the realities of its species. The specific requirement prevailing upon them will make its fullest appearance. The specific form of man, for example, requires that an individual being should have two hands, two feet and two eyes, etc., but what happens that, at times, matter is found incapable of producing twofold limbs, thus, the child born is either lame, or one-eyed, etc. Here the fault is of the matter and not of the specific form. Similarly, in matters relating to the non-material life; the specific form requires that man should have sound reason, should be free from impurity of false ideas, so that he could acquire true knowledge from God; and it also requires that his imaginative power should be developed enough to shape things according to the nature of the Similitudinary World (*'Ālam-ul-Mithāl*).[12]

In short, individual qualities will vanish and the specific form will dominate and will be reflected by man's intellectual and imaginative faculties, and there the individual being will manifest the specific requirements so well and complete that a better manifestation than that would not be possible. This is the same state to which the Qur'ān refers: "Thou wast heedless of this; now have We removed thy veil, and sharp is thy sight this Day."[13]

The Similitudinary World is a world full of knowledge, which does not admit of any ignorance, omission or neglect. It is a clear exposition of the World of Souls (*'Ālam-ul-Arwāḥ*) and is encompassing everything of this material world, great and small. Here the similitudinary sciences are revealed to man and he himself becomes a representative of the World of Similitudes itself. The changes which are to come upon

12. *Ḥujjatullāh*, Vol. I, pp. 36-38; *Tafhimāt*, Vol. I, p. 253.

13. *Ḥujjatullāh*, Vol. I, pp. 36-37; *Tafhimāt*, Vol. I. p. 253; *Saṭa'āt*, *Saṭa'* 25. Sūrah Qāf, verse 23.

him there would, however, correspond to his attraction towards the realities of that world (*'Ālam-ul-Mithāl*). If his *Nasmah* retained signs of good qualities, he will see the similitudinary changes very clearly, otherwise they will appear to him dim and incomplete. But the scenes which he will see there would not be a dream or a fancy but a reality and an established truth.

If we were to describe the World of Similitudes (ideas) in an ordinary language we would rather say that it is a material world, but refined beyond all refinement, absolutely pure and immune from the dirt of the bodies of this material world, and it would be said on that day as the Qur'ān puts it: "the heaven and the earth have changed." [14]

The thing to be borne in mind here is that the regathering of bodies and the infusion of souls in them is not a new life. The other-worldly life is the completion of the worldly life, and the relation between them is like that of the cause and effect. If we take it for granted, that resurrection (*ḥashr*) is a new life, it would follow that men who will have the blessing of life there would be other than those who were once moving about here. If that be so, the question of reward or punishment does not arise, as this would be against the law of cause and effect. The thing made the second time would still be the original one, but greatly transformed. Likewise the body man would be given on the Judgment Day for the second

14. *Al-Budūr-ul-Bāzighah*, p. 153. Sūrah Ibrāhīm, verse 48.

time would not be exactly the same as he had it before, because of its great transformation. It would be just the middle of the material and the non-material.[15]

On the Judgment Day, man is to account for his actions which were the result of the faculties of his heart (*Qalbīyah*); he will not be held responsible for those actions that proceeded from him in consequence of his temperamental (*Ṭab'īyah*) and apprehensive (*Idrākīyah*) faculties, like greed and jealousy, etc., which are only a tale of man's thought and mind, and which do not stick to the root of the soul, nor will he be questioned for actions which he did under emergencies, and actions which arose out of hypocrisy, publicity and pride, etc. The things which are to harm him on that Day are his denial of the truth, his spreading of mischief in the land, his ignorance of God and the lack of his attention towards Him.[16]

Imām Ghazālī has warned against the consequences of every ignoble act, but the fact, Shāh Ṣāḥib says, is that the man will be rewarded only for those of his actions which had clung to the very root of his *Nasmah*, and continued to remain with it even after his death as is clear in the verse of the poet Jamīl. There his angelic aspect will prevail and the animal

15. *Ḥujjatullāh*, Vol. I, pp. 19, 36-37 ; *Tafhimāt*, Vol. I, p. 61 :

... ثم اذا جاء وقت الحساب والسؤال حولت ابدانهم نورية الى بين المثال والناسوت ۔

16. *Al-Budūr-ul-Bāzighah*, p. 152 : *Tafhimāt*, Vol. I, p. 250 :

... تا اراده و اختيار عبد در كار نباشد نفس ناطقه رنگ فعل را در خود نكشد و سببيت جزاء منعقد نگردد ۔

one will remain dormant.[17]

Some philosophers are of opinion that the anima aspect will vanish after death, but according to Shāl Walīyullāh, the *Nasmah* will continue to survive unti man's life in Paradise.[18]

Balance and Bridge. There the actions of man would be weighed in the Balance, and he would be made to pass over the Bridge, sharper than a sword's blade and thinner than a hair.

By this Bridge is meant the straight path of the *Sharī'ah* (*al-Ṣirāṭ-ul-Mustaqīm*), which will appear there in the material form. In explaining the words of God: "This is My path, the right, straight one, so follow it and do not follow the other paths," the Holy Prophet had drawn a straight line, round which were drawn some curved ones. The Bridge, as a matter of fact, is the sample of that order (way of life) which is implanted in the nature of men and their difference in crossing it is also due to their difference in following that order. The man who follows the path of the *Sharī'ah* strictly will pass over that Bridge like a lightning.[19]

As for the Balance, it is the representation of the actions of man, after the type of the matter of the World of Ideas (*'Ālam-ul-Mithāl*), that is to say, the Balance will appear in a material form, but

17. *Al-Budūr-ul-Bāzighah*, pp. 146-48, 234 : *Tafhimāt*, Vol. II, p. 61. Sūrah al-An'ām, verse 154. *Al-Budūr-ul-Bāzighah*, p. 148 :

اريد لا'نسى ذكرها فكأنما   تمثل لى ليلى فى كل سبيل

18. *Tafhimāt*, Vol. I, p. 166; 'Ubaidullāh Sindhī, *al-Maqām-ul-Maḥmūd*, p. 54.

19. *Al-Khair-ul-Kathir*, pp. 114-15; *Tafhimāt*, Vol. I, p. 254.

neither purely material nor non-material, rather just in between. In other words, the material objects will appear in the shape of non-material ones. From the attributes of God, one is His discriminatory knowledge, which is to make distinction between right and wrong. On that Day, this attribute will be reflected in the form of a Balance, which will separate the good from evil.

Reckoning and Fountain. Reckoning (*Ḥisāb*) is also one of the manifestations of His attribute of discernment which will appear at the time of the setting up of the Balance in a way a thing is weighed in a balance in this world, but this phase would be momentary, as the words of God make it clear: "God is very quick in taking account."[20]

By the Fountain (*Kauthar*) is meant the guidance of the Holy Prophet which he received from God, and which he disseminated in the world. It will take the shape of water, because there is a very close resemblance between water and guidance. Every prophet will have his own fountain, but the fountain of the Holy Prophet will be the source of all. He who followed the *Sharī'ah* properly will drink the brimful cups from it, and he who obeyed it less will have proportionately less of it.[21]

The Holy Prophet has said that God has given him a river in the Paradise. It is whiter than milk, sweeter than honey and is as vast as is the distance

20. *Al-Khair-ul-Kathīr*, p. 113; *Tafhīmāt*, Vol. I, pp. 253-54. Sūrah al-Baqarah, verse 202.
21. *Al-Khair-ul-Kathīr*, p. 114; *Tafhīmāt*, Vol. I, p. 254.

between east and west. Whosoever drank from it once will never feel thirsty again and one who performed ablution from it will never become dirty.

Paradise is the manifestation of the amiable (*Jamālī*) attributes of God, while Hell is the manifestation of His terrible (*Jalālī*) attributes. The manifestation of His amiable attributes will be represented in the form of beautiful-eyed damsels (*Ḥūr*), stately palaces, delicious foods and drinks and splendid garments, while the manifestation of His terrible attributes will assume the shape of things contrary to them.[22]

A'rāf. On that Day, people will be divided into various classes. One class would be that of the "right-handed" which again is of many kinds, but it includes all those persons who performed good actions. Among them one group is named "the inmates of *A'rāf* (the boundary between Paradise and Hell)." It includes persons who had neither done any good, nor had committed any evil; and if they did any good at all, they did it as a formality or on account of some custom, and were very negligent. God, after taking their account, will forgive them and send them to Paradise.[23]

Among the inmates of *A'rāf*, there will be people who did not receive the message of God, and also those living on the mountain-tops who neither believed in Him nor associated anything with Him, and were just like animals who care only for the satisfac-

22. *Al-Khair-ul-Kathīr*, p. 115; *al-Budūr-ul-Bāzighah*, p. 154; *Saṭa'āt*, *Saṭa'* 41; *Ilhām-ur-Raḥmān*, p. 29.
23. *Al-Budūr-ul-Bāzighah*, p. 157.

tion of their natural requirements. And if at all they received the message of Islam they did not derive any benefit from it, due to their ignorance. They failed to understand the Qur'ān and its arguments. They were bred and brought up under circumstances which prevented them from paying any attention to deep thinking. They were capable of only this much knowledge that the Muslims are a people who eat such and such things and consider such and such things as forbidden; and who fight with others for the sake of conquering their country, and as such, they should also fight with them. As these people were like quadrupeds and had not associated anything with God, they would not be blamed or taken to task, even though they had been normal in their nature otherwise.

Among the inmates of *A'rāf* would also be included persons who were deficient in reason, and were unable to make distinction between right and wrong; and they, on account of their deficient power of thinking, were not able to know God and remember Him, such as children, lunatics, imbeciles, fools and rustics. They were, however, expected to have only as much of belief as was found in that negro slave-woman who, when asked by the Holy Prophet about God, had pointed out to the Heaven above; the Prophet thereat had remarked that she was a believer.[24]

24 *Al-Budūr-ul-Bāzighah*, pp. 163-64; *Ḥujjatullāh*, Vol. I, pp. 25, 116-17:
اصحاب الاعراف جنسان قوم صحت امز جتہم و زکت فطرتہم و لم تبلغہم الدعوة الاسلامیة اصلا ، او بلغتہم ولاکن بنحو لا تقوم به الحجة ـ ـ ـ و قوم نقصت عقولہم کاکثر الصبیان و المعتوهین و الفلاحین والارقاء ـ ـ

Besides, those to whom the message of the new faith (*Sharī'ah*, Islam) had not been conveyed and explained properly and their doubts had not been cleared would not be punished from the *Sharī'ah's* side. They also will be lodged in *A'rāf*.[25]

Shāh Ṣāḥib, as has already been mentioned, was an extraordinary genius in the art of removing the apparent discrepancies of the text. Here is an example of it.

At certain places in the text is found that the doer of a great sin and the one against whom stands the payment of the debts of others will not be forgiven, while at some other places the contents of the text run quite opposite to that.

Shāh Ṣāḥib removes this discrepancy by saying that God Almighty works in two ways: one is the common, and the other, under certain conditions, is the uncommon one. As such, according to the latter way, their forgiveness is possible.[26]

The progress of man does not end with his life in Paradise. There is still a higher and nobler stage before him, for the acquisition of which he always aspires and remains restless. After his stay for quite a long time in Paradise, his *Nasmah* will become weak, and will go on shaping itself from every point of view according to the requirement of the soul (*Nafs*

25. *Ḥujjatullāh*, Vol. I, p. 25:

و أما المجازاة بالوجه الرابع (من جانب الشرع) فلا تكون الا بعد بعثة الانبياء و كشف الشبهة و صحة التبليغ -

26. *Ḥusn-ul-'Aqīdah.*

Nāṭiqah), until it attains its ultimate aim. His progress after death depends upon the disintegration of his *Nasmah*, and a time will come when he would eventually be changed into the divine or the angelic soul.[27]

Rūḥ-i-Samāwī. When God intended to create man, there appeared a human form in a way to conform to every human individual. The soul (*nafs*) of the *'Arsh*, by which in *Sharī'ah* is meant "the World of *Dhikr* (World of Similitudes)," accepted that human form and in its wake it was accepted by all the other souls of the celestial bodies as well, until it (the whole) became a form suspended, standing in the Heavenly world, and looked as if it is standing without any support. This looked like the presence of too many lamps when their lights intermingle, and then it becomes difficult to trace every light to its individual lamp. Thereafter certain celestial conditions required that the Universal human form (humanity) should become clear in every individual in a manner they (the celestial conditions) and the earthly capabilities require that time. It then became so represented that if a man were to appear in this particular condition and with this capability, then "this" would be the soul, and if he were to appear in that particular condition and with that capability, then "that" would be the soul.[28]

Ultimate Goal. Shāh Walīyullāh explains this as follows: "The body of man is only a cover for the

27. *Al-Budūr-ul-Bāzighah*, p. 140; *al-Khair-ul-Kathīr*, p. 93; *Ilhām-ur Rahmān*, p. 29; *Anfās-ul-'Ārifīn*, p. 77.

28. *Tafhīmāt*, Vol. I, pp. 247-48.

soul, and his *Nasmah* is filled with the power of the 'Ideal World' (Similitudinary World). It is, therefore, that this *Nasmah* is preserved. The Holy Qur'ān says: 'There is no soul but has a protector over it.'[29] As a star preserves its light intact, similarly, the power of the World of Ideas preserves the *Nasmah* and keeps it safe and commands full domination over every part of it. *Nasmah* is just like a paper, on which the actions of man when performed deliberately are imprinted and are protected against obliteration by the power of the 'Ideal World'. This is how humanity is preserved. Besides the power of the World of Ideas, there are other powers also which influence the *Nasmah*. One of them is the angelic power, a light of the Sublime Assembly (*al-Mala'-ul-A'lā'*) the origin of which is the Holy Fold (*Ḥaẓīrat ul-Quds*). This angelic power is strongly connected with the *Nasmah*. The other power that influences the *Nasmah* is the Rational Soul (*Nafs Nāṭiqah*), which is the reflection of the original source of the human species (*Imām-i-Nau'-i-Insān*). With the loss of body, no action of man is lost. As the serpent casts off its slough, similarly the soul replaces this bodily dress with another one. After a very long time, disintegration will set in the *Nasmah* and a time will come when it will be replaced by the power of the 'World of Ideas'; and when with the passage of time it also will become weak, the man which it used to protect will come under the protection of the angel ic power. But after a long time when the angelic

29. Sūrah aṭ-Ṭāriq, verse 4.

power will also weaken, man and his faculties will come under the protection of the Divine Soul. Ultimately, he will reach the central point of *ash-Shakhṣ-ul-Akbar*. On this point, the part of which he will eventualy become, the Great Emanation (*Tajallī al-A'ẓam*) is constantly reflected This is man's union with God and his oneness with Him." [30]

Here it should be remembered that the central point in *ash-Shakhṣ-ul-Akbar* combines all the parts of the Universe. It is more fine, more resembling to pure incorporeality and is more suitable to become its mirror. The real cause of the particularisation of this point for becoming the mirror of the Truth (God) is the Divine Providence. This central point is for God as the nest is for the bird.[31]

30. *Al-Budūr-ul-Bāzighah*, p. 140 ; *Saṭa'āt, Saṭa'* 29 :
و چون بدن نسمی متناثر شدن گرفت هر قدرکه متناثر می شد اعتماد نفس منصرف می گشت و همان قدر به سطح مثال اعتماد می گرفت و طبقات مثال متفاوت است اعلی همه همین نکته بسیط وحدانی است که در تمام شخص اکبر معین است . . . آخر تصاعد طبیعی این است که به این نکته برسد ۔ چون ماده باین نقطه رسید و صورت کائنه در آئینه با ''تجلی اعظم'' یکی گشت سفر طویل تمام شد ۔

31. *Saṭa'āt, Saṭa'* 7.

Chapter X

PHILOSOPHY

THE Greeks were the first people who took interest in the science of philosophy. Aristotle was the foremost among them. He was a man of sound mind and clear brain, and was considerably inclined towards ascertaining the truth. After the advent of Islam, Ḥunain translated the Greek philosophy into Arabic, and then the Muslims began to show interest in it. Abū 'Alī Sīnā attempted, though unsuccessfully, to bring a compromise between the Islamic and the Greek philosophies. He wrote on philosophy with great skill and care, and brought out a book, *ash-Shifā'*, but, if that philosophy be examined thoroughly, it would be found rather weak and deficient in the explanation of the essence and attributes of God; and his observations on this subject were a sheer supposition and a guess work.[1]

Shāh Ṣāḥib regrets that the Muslim is not giving his thought and is not turning his eyes towards the vast world around him, though his latent faculties do aspire to conquer the earth and the heaven and what is between the two. Until and unless he pays attention to it with unusual zeal and enthusiasm, and continues his efforts and makes some remarkable progress

1. *As-Sirr-ul-Maktūm fi Asbāb Tadwin-il-'Ulūm* :
و أنت ان فتشت الحال و جدته أضعف شئ فى مباحث الالاه و
صفاته - - - -

in this direction, he himself and his religion (Islam) will remain in the secondary position, and the complete prevalence of Islam which was the main purpose of the advent of the Holy Prophet will not be achieved. This was the chief cause of his anxiety, and he, therefore, cleansed the rational science from all the muddy admixture and clearly manifested the weakness of Greek philosophy which had become current in those days.[2]

If one were to read Shāh Ṣāḥib carefully, one will find in him one distinguishing quality, namely, whenever he discusses a particular topic, he always makes a rational approach towards it. For example, while speaking on the subject of "virtue and vice," he asserts that a thing can be said to be good only when it abounds in the exhibition of its specific characteristics. The more a thing is near to its species, the better it is, and the more it is wanting in its specific characteristics, the farther is it removed from good. When it is said that such and such a horse is good, it is always meant thereby that its specific characteristics are perfectly manifested by it, and not that it is superior to man. Man is also said to be good when he demonstrates his specific characteristics to a greater extent. The question, however, arises as to what are the characteristics of man which can serve as a standard!

A philosopher will surely say that all the people of the world should be taken into consideration. Whatever

2. *Tafhīmāt*, Vol. I, p. 214 ; *al-Juz'-ul-Laṭīf*.

good attributes be found common among them should form the composite elements of humanity. This definition of virtue and vice goes by the name of *Fiṭrah* which is not subject to any change. The laws of *Fiṭrah* deal with the principles and universals of virtue and vice and not with their consequences and particulars. And this is the standard by which every man or group can be tested. By defining "virtue and vice" in this manner, the importance of action emerges more clearly than that of the thought. In establishing any action or belief to be good, Shāh Ṣāḥib generally looks from the point as to whether it is shared by the majority of the people the world over. This idea of Shāh Ṣāḥib is indeed a most valuable one.[3]

In philosophy, the problem of existence (*wujūd*, being) is very important and delicate. Shāh Ṣāḥib gives an explanation of it as follows:

"When we look at the universe, we find two things in it: one is partnership and the other is separation. Human beings, for example, are partners in humanity, and are separate from each other by virtue of their varying peculiarities and shapes. Similarly, all the living creatures are partners of each other as life is common among all of them, while the thing which is common among all that is in the Universe is the existence. This is, however, found both in the possible (*Mumkin*) and in the necessary (*Wājib*). But by existence is not meant its verbal meaning; what is meant by it is its reality, on the strength of which a thing is called existent. This reality, however, exists indepen-

3. *Ḥujjatullāh*, Vol. I, pp. 50-51, 58:

و ليس ذالک الا فی اصول البر والاثم و کلیاتها دون فروعها و حدودها

و هذه الفطرة هوالدين لا يختلف باختلاف الزمان ۔

Maulānā 'Ubaidullāh Sindhī, *Shāh Walīyullāh aur Un kā Falsafah*, pp. 24-27

dent of any creator, and as such, it is the source of all existence and must exist before every existence. This existence embraces all, and a thing outside it is a sheer nonentity. Accordingly, the existence of all other things is not real but relative. If it exists, everything exists, and if it were to cease to exist, everything will cease to exist. This existence, therefore, is the very person of God and all that exists in the Universe exists because of this." [4]

It should not, however, be imagined that the Primal One (God) is one individual of the being (existence) and the being has included it as the whole includes its individual parts. Nay, the Primal One has encompassed this universal conception of the being (whether in the external world or in the world of realities, which is only an extraction, an idea, that has no meaning save that it is represented in the brain) from above, from below and from all its sides. It is so, because this conception of the being is taken only when those realities which are the source of many different effects are briefly considered, and in this way it (being) is distinguished from the not-being, but its (Primal One's) reality is not distinguished from the other realities; and what is more right to regard is that Reality (*Ḥaqīqat-ul-Wujūd*). It should not, however, be taken as a substance or a genus or anything of that kind. The relation of everything, when it is to be related to the One, is like the relation the number one has with the cardinal numbers. But by that relation is meant that one precedes two and is present in every number.[5]

Pantheism and Apparenticism. In the writings of

4. *Maktūb-i-Madani.*
5. *Lamaḥāt, Lamḥah* 2-3, 8-9.

Shaikh-i-Akbar, Ibn-ul-'Arabī, both these ideas are found. Sometimes he calls the Universe the person of God, and takes everything in it as self-existent, and at times he believes Him to be quite outside the Universe. The scholars, on this account, have been confused as to the real object of the Shaikh. Imām Rabbānī Mujaddid Alif-i-Thānī presented the idea of Apparenticism (*Waḥdat-ush-Shuhūd*), against the idea of the unity of Being (*Waḥdat-ul-Wujūd*). Shāh Walīyullāh has endeavoured to effect a compromise between the two and has shown that the difference between them is only of the form and not of the substance. He explains it as follows: Zaid, 'Amr and Bakr, from one point of view, share the same personality, because humanity is common in them, as they are all human beings. Similarly, the human species and the animal species are the same from this point of view that life is commonly shared by both. Similarly, this Universe has also a soul (*nafs*) as an individual being has a soul. This Universal Soul (*an-Nafs-ul-Kullīyah*) is the genus of all genera, and is also called by some mystics the "Self-unfolding Existence" (*al-Wujūd-ul-Munbasiṭ*). It is, however, the nature of this existence that it penetrates and pervades everything, but, in spite of that, it is outside the phenomena. It is both immanent and transcendental. The relation which this Universe has with the Universal Soul is approximately similar to the relation this Universal Soul has with the Self-Existent (God); but the Universal Soul, in spite of its being near to the Universe, is not so far away from it as the Self-Existent is far away from it (the Universal Soul).

The Universal Soul embraces both the substance and the accident and is capable of taking the form of both. The belief of the Greek philosophers that there is no common genus over and above the substance and the accident is not correct. They, however, do not believe in it, as it cannot be proved by reason, and according to them a thing which cannot be proved by reason should not be accepted or taken for granted. Contrary to these philosophers, Shāh Ṣāḥib's observation is that the Reality is one and the same, but that it appears in two forms. When it appears in the original form of its existence, it is called the "substance," and when it manifests itself in the form of other existence, it is called the "accident".[6]

In short, after deep thinking over the Universe, man has come to the conclusion that there is a Universal Soul from which this whole Universe has emanated. According to Shāh Walīyullāh, this Universal Soul has again emanated from God by way of invention (*bi-ṭarīq-i-ibdā'*). In other words, the relation which exists between God and the Universal Soul is that of invention and not of creation; and by *ibdā'* is meant a relation which is known by its essentiality (*annīyyah*, ecceity), but is unknown to its quality and is beyond

6. *Saṭa'āt*, *Saṭa'* 5; *Alṭāf-ul-Quds*, p. 104; *Shāh Walīyullāh aur Un kā Falsafah*, pp. 68-70:

درمیان مُبدِع و مُبدَع نسبتی واقع است ... معلوم الآنية مجهول الكيفية ـ

the reach of reason.[7]

Obviously, it refers to this fact that God is far away from this Universe. Shāh Ṣāḥib says that the relation which exists between the inventor (*Mubdi'*) and the invented (*Mubda'*) is not such as could be explained by some simile or parable, nor is it of that kind of unity according to which it could be said that this preceded and that one succeeded, or that, from the point of time, this one was prior to the other one. Thus, the substance of this whole is that there is some sort of unity between God and the Universal Soul, but that unity is not real. The human intellect, however, can reach the Universal Soul, but it cannot move a step further. It is quite unable to understand the relation of invention (*Ibdā'*) that exists between the two and is helpless to make any distinction in them. It is, therefore, that, at times, God and the Universal Soul are taken to be one and the same thing.[8]

As has already been mentioned, the Universal Soul (or *al-Wujūd-ul-Munbasiṭ*) is both inside and outside the objects of Nature, and it is this existence to which allusion is made in the external in our saying "Zaid is in the external world" and it is this same existence hinted at in the realities in our saying "Zaid

7. *Alṭāf-ul-Quds*, pp. 104-05 ; *Hama'āt, Hāma'* 13 :
بر این فقیر مشخص ساخته اند که آن حقیقت که مطمح ایشان درین شده است ، نفس کلیه است ، و همان است آنکه بعض مکاشفین وجود منبسط نیز نامند ۔ ۔ ۔ این وجود باوجود سریان وی در اشیاء و قرب وی بآنها از همه پاکست و از جمیع الواث منزهٔ صد چند آن ذات الهیه ازین نفس کلیه دور است ۔

8. *Alṭāf-ul-Quds*, p. 107; *al-Khair-ul-Kathīr*, p. 39.

is in the realities (*A'yān*)," and it is equally the same existence pointed out in the actualisation when we say "Zaid is actualised after he was not." Why should it not be like that ? Everything existing in the external and in the realities is already preceded by the external and the realities, and every actualised thing is preceded by its actuality. In short, existence is common, both in God and in the Universe, and this has led some mystics to the conclusion that God means the Universe ; and the reference of the Shaikh (Ibn-ul-'Arabi), when he speaks of the "unity of being," is also to this existence (*al-Wujūd-ul-Munbasiṭ*), as it agrees to both, the Universe (*Taḥaqquq*) and God. The Ultimate Reality is, however, still far away.[9]

Here, Shāh Ṣāḥib finds a point of agreement between various religions. The Christians assert that the Divinity has appeared in the dress of man, and the Hindus are of the belief that the perfect men are the incarnation of God Himself.

God, in dispelling their doubt, said in the Holy Qur'ān : "Verily We strengthened him (Jesus) through the Holy Spirit." By the Holy Spirit, says Shāh Ṣāḥib, is meant here the Great Emanation (*at-Tajallī al-A'ẓam*) and its "strengthening" points to the constant overflow of its blessings on that man in whom its shadow takes a certain form in a way, it appears,

9. *Maktūb-i-Madani* :
فکذالک الصوفیة یقولون العالم عین الحق یعنون عینیة کله فی الوجود المنبسط و قیام الوجود المنبسط بالحق الاول ۔

as if he is the Great Emanation Itself.[10]

Explaining further he says that this Great Emanation takes place in the world at a time particularly when the people come under the overweaning presumption that the Divinity has put on the dress of a human being and that the Truth has entered into (*ḥulūl*) some perfect minds.

But as time passed, many a misunderstanding arose in the minds of people and they began to take Jesus and other holy persons as the incarnation of God or an embodiment of the Great Emanation (*at-Tajallī al-A'ẓam*) which was a gross ignorance and a folly, as they took the shadow of Reality as Reality Itself.

The claim as advanced by the late Maulānā 'Ubaidullāh Sindhī that he could effect an agreement between the world religions on the basis of Shāh Walīyullāh's philosophy finds some justification in the example given above.[11]

The philosophy of Shāh Walīyullāh is spread over in his various works. There is no systematic treatment of it as a whole at one place. There are, however, his two famous treatises *Lamaḥāt* and *Saṭa'āt* where some continuity is maintained. It is, therefore, that his grandson Shāh Ismā'īl Shahīd collected the relative material and explained it clearly in his book *'Abaqāt*.

Ash-Shakhṣ-ul-Akbar. It should be known that

10. *Lamaḥāt, Lamḥah* 58 ; *al-Fauz-ul-Kabīr*, pp. 9-10 ; *Saṭa'āt, Saṭa'* 45. Surah al-Baqarah, verse 87.

11. Maulānā 'Ubaidullāh Sindhī, *Dhāti Diary*, pp. 26-27.

ash-Shakhṣ-ul-Akbar is the all in all (minus God), whether the greatest of the bodies which, in the terminology of the philosophers, is called the Primum Mobile (*Falak-ul-Aflāk*), whether the other celestial spheres, the Sublime Assembly (*Mala'-i-A'lā*), the Lower Assemly (*Mala'-i-Sāfil*) of the angels or the species of the animal. All of them are replete with the similitudinary power (*Quwwat-i-Mithālīyah*), as if it has stuffed the whole of the Universe. One covering is the essence (*nafs*) and the other is the corporealities and it (the similitudinary power) has fallen in between these two. This whole body, namely, *ash-Shakhṣ-ul-Akbar*, is an independent matter in itself, and the other different bodies which it contains are like the waves in its ocean. This body carries with itself a temperamental power, the function of which is to change and transform the various parts of the body according to their suitable forms and shapes, and it is called the Univeral Temperament (*aṭ-Ṭabī'at-ul-Kullīyah*). As every man has a soul, similarly that big body also has a soul, which is called the Universal Soul. The relation of the souls of different bodies with this soul is similar to the relation the faculties of seeing, hearing and thinking have with the soul of man. Or their relation with it is like the relation the embryo has with its mother when they both are mixed up with each other. It (*ash-Shakhṣ-ul-Akbar*) is the origin of both time and space, capable of changes infinitely. Now, this big body with all its powers is named *ash-Shakhṣ-ul-Akbar* (the Universe).

The work of the Creator of the forms is, firstly

to create the origin, namely, the Great Body (the Universe) which is compounded of two powers, active and passive; secondly, to create all things which are ingrained in the Great Body's nature *(Isti'dād)*: and, thirdly, to preserve all those things as long as it survives. Consequently, the extent of emanation from it (the Creator) would be to illumine this at one time and to illumine that at another time. Its continuous emanation from the First (God) is, however, necessary for its own continuation. This is what becomes the Great Body.

Now if one, after having reached the Great Body, were to incline to the side of the Real *(al-Ḥaqq)*, one will find that the Great Body does not emanate from It, but is always there with It. And if one were to incline from the side of the Real towards the Great Body one will find that the Great Body and none else emanates from It (the Real), and yet this same Great Body is there with It and this same one is *an-Nafs-ul-Kullīyah* (or *al Wujūd-ul-Munbasiṭ*, which is capable of assuming different forms). This (Universal Soul) would be found there as established and real, without an equal and without any rival in its rank, but absolutely unique, because here both the Being (God) and the Universe are in agreement. Everything attributed, as having emanated from It (the Real), is in fact attributed to it. (the Great Body), because of the latter's being mingled up with the former. It was, however, brought into existence simply by the will of God, that is to say, by way of invention (*bi-tarīq-i-ibdā'*). He who believes that the Great Body is the first emanation is correct; and the "First Intellect" in essence is also the Great Body itself and this Great Body is a name and a frontispiece of God.[12]

'Ālam-i-Mithāl. Every little or great thing, for example even the worm, has its own imaginative power, and this is so because *ash-Shakhṣ-ul-Akbar* has a great power of imagination, which is called *'Ālam-i-Mithāl* (World of Similitudes—of Ideas). Its relation to the Great Body is like the relation of the well-arranged bodies (designs) to the imagination of an architect. However, when looked at the procession of the effects, the Great Body is called the Universal Temperament, and every other soul (*nafs*) as a particular temperament. From those particular souls, the one which is nearest to incorporeality (*tajarrud*) is named the World of Spirits, and that which is remotest from incorporeality is given the name of the visible world; while that which is in the intermediate is termed as the World of Similitudes (Ideal World).[13]

Similarly, the World of Ideas, even though in relation to *ash-Shakhṣ-ul-Akbar*, is but an idea or an image (*khayāl*), but if a man does not look at *ash-Shakhṣ-ul-Akbar* from different points of view, and

12. *Saṭa'āt, Saṭa'* 6; *Lamaḥāt, Lamḥah* 16, 19-21, 24:

فاذا انحدرت اليها (النفس الكلية) وجدتها متقررا متحققا ليس لها ند ولا ضد فى درجتها بل شاذة لوفق الوجود والتحقق ـ

'Abaqāt, 'Abaqah 10:

والنفس الكلية و هو غير نفس الكل التى هى النفس المتعلقة بالعرش ـ

Maulānā 'Ubaidullāh Sindhī, *Urdu Sharḥ-i-Ḥujjatullāh*, pp. 75-77.

13. *Saṭa'āt, Saṭa'* 3; *Lamaḥāt, Lamḥah* 24; Maulānā 'Ubaidullah Sindhī, *Urdu Sharḥ-i-Ḥujjatullāh*, pp. 75-77.

then bring it under his consideration as a whole, he will certainly find that the "World of Ideas" is the real world, so much so that he will begin to feel it even more lasting than this material world. He will see then that the things which are present here are already present there in that world, and here they are merely their reflection and a shadow. And he who does not believe in the existence of the *'Ālam-i-Mithāl* is certainly not from the rightly-guided (*Ahl-us-Sunnah*).[14]

However, there exists in the Universe a World of Ideas, which is not made of matter and is super-material. This is a world in which the ideas and actions of men assume suitable forms, and every happening which is to happen in the material world is to happen there first. Everything was in some way already in existence in that world, and then it became correct to say about it that this thing is exactly thesame as was seen in the World of Ideas. According to one Tradition, the Chapters al-Baqarah and Āl-i-'Imrān will appear on the Judgment Day in the form of two clouds or in the shape of two flocks of birds. They will then intercede for their constant readers. There is a mention in another Tradition that the world, on the Judgment Day, would be brought in the shape of an old, ugly woman with dim (blue) eyes and projected teeth. Besides, there is the Tradition that the angels are striking the dead man in the grave with iron hammers, and the man raises

14. *'Abaqāt*, pp. 219 20 :
الجاحد بالوجود المثالى ليس من أهل السنة حقا بل فيه شوب من الاعتزال -

cries which are heard everywhere (but not by men and Jinn). For an unbeliever, ninety-nine snakes are let loose which continue biting him until the Judgment Day. There are many Traditions similar to these giving the proof of the existence of the World of Ideas.[15]

Shāh Walīyullāh is of the belief that the Traditions with regard to the "World of Ideas" be taken literally and their interpretations may be avoided.[16]

Hazīrat-ul-Quds (*The Holy Fold*). One of the basic principles in the philosophy of Shāh Walīyullāh is the doctrine of the "Holy Fold". All the Divine Grace, which flows from the Throne of God towards mankind, flows through the agency of the "Holy Fold". It is the origin of many of the events, particularly the important ones which take place in the world, like the advent of the prophet and the establishment of new nations, etc. It is a spiritual place where the angels near to the Throne of God and the spirits of the perfect men meet together. Their meeting produces a flood of light forming a circle (like the halo around the moon) for "the Soul" (*Rūḥ*). Their combination is named the "Hold Fold".

In reference to that Soul, the Holy Prophet has said that it has as many faces and tongues as the people have. This Soul is that existence which is called the Origin of mankind (*Imām-i-Nau'-i-Insān, Insān-i-Kabīr, Tajallī Ilāhī*).

All the souls of men are derived from that Great Soul which is in the shape of a man. As the rays of

15. *Ḥujjatullāh*, Vol. I, pp. 13-14.
16. Ibid.

the sun radiate from the sun and after illuminating the earth return to the sun, similarly all the individual souls emanate from that Great Soul, come to the world, and after finishing their job go back to merge in it, and through it they maintain their connection with their Lord. On the Judgment Day, this "Great Soul" will attract these individual souls to itself as the magnet attracts the iron.

It is mentioned in the *Sharī'ah* that there are some angels of a very high rank, who are very near to God. They are bearing His Throne and are praying to Him for the believers all the time. They have no other occupation save the remembrance of their Lord, and are not heedless of Him even for a moment. One of their official duties is to perform the job of envoys between God and His servants, and are always inspiring into the hearts of people the thoughts to do good and avoid evil. The following verse points to that fact that the souls of the pious and the God-fearing join those angels after death : "O (thou) soul, in (complete) rest and satisfaction come back thou, to thy Lord, well pleased (thyself), and well pleasing unto Him. Enter thou, then, among My devotees, yea enter thou My heaven."[17]

The final goal of man's progress is his attainment of a certain part of the plane of the "Holy Fold," which has already been fixed for him.[18]

17. *Ḥujjatullāh*, Vol. I, p. 16 ; *Tafhīmāt*, Vol. I, p. 65. Surah Fajr, verses 27-30.

18. *Saṭa'āt, Saṭa'* 34:

و مقرر پیش فقیر آن است که مطلوب وصول است بجزی از سطح
حظیرةالقدس که برائی او مقرر ساخته اند -

Here below is reproduced a rather detailed account of the "Holy Fold" which is an exact copy of the image of God, as given by Shāh Ṣāḥib in his *Lamaḥāt*:

"Now, if you want to reach the farthest limit of its (Holy Fold's) reality, then know that there are many points in every particular soul, and in opposition to every point there are particular attributes and effects, and they (points) have an origin which necessitates them. And though the case of these points at the very outset appears to be confusing, the deep thinking which pays the due right to every rightful one does not mix up one thing with the other. For example, the human individual is a speaking and white one, etc. When you see every man a speaking one, you are led to the conclusion that the point which makes the speech necessary is common in all the human individuals, and we find that there is many a stone which is white and there is many a man who is black. Thus, that point is other than the one by which he speaks even though they both, the stone and man, meet together by coincidence at one and the same place. Similarly, the universal soul has many points in opposition to every state which is to come upon it one day in its lifetime. From its points is one which happens to be in opposition to reality (*Taḥaqquq*, the point of view of the Real) and actuality. This point is the very image of the Being whose existence is necessary, is its manifestation and its exact copy. This is the origin of the Holy Fold. When the celestial spheres came into existence along with their knowledge and powers, the first thing they conceived of was the Being whose existence was necessary. His form was such that all their knowledge agreed on it And when there is neither any ignorance nor any kind of confusion, it became necessary that that form of the Being should tally with those points to a certain extent. And this is the first appearance of the Holy Fold. Again, when the causes required that the superior angels and the knowing selves joined with them be brought into existence, they by the very essence of their nature were forced to incline to this Holy Fold as inclines every creature to its object of inclination. When they (angels and selves) joined that point, encompassed it, submitted to it and humbled themselves before it, they acquired certain attributes according to their capabilities (*Isti'dādāt*). Consequently, the circle of the Holy Fold became enlarged. This Holy Fold, even though it has no particular place or location from the point of space, the nearest interpretation of it is this that it is the *Raḥmān* sitting on the Throne (*'Arsh*), the angels of the high rank (*al-Mala'-ul-A'lā*—the Sublime Assembly) are bearing it (that Throne) and the execution (*Qaḍā'*) proceeds from here."[19]

He who came to know of the Holy Fold, through the glass of his own reality, namely, through the form of humanity, unavoidably began to say that "God created Adam after His form" and that it (Holy Fold) loves all what the nature (*Fiṭrah*) of man requires, and what is suitable to it and is profitable for it, and that it dislikes all that is repugnant to the requirements of man's nature.[20]

It indeed goes to the credit of Shāh Walīyullāh that he brought philosophy near to the understanding of the common man. As by philosophy he does neces-

19. *Lamaḥāt, Lamḥah* 32. By *Raḥmān*, in the philosophy of Shāh Walīyullāh, is meant the manifestation of the person of God on the Throne in the same manner as the human form is reflected in the mirror.

'Abaqāt, 'Abaqah 21, p. 110 :

– – – وحظيرة القدس صارت تجليا واحدا مظهر الجمال وجه الله الكريم تفصيلا ، فهذا التجلى المنبسط هو المحبوب فى الحقيقة لكل محب والمعشوق لكل عاشق –

20. *'Abaqāt : Ishārah* II, *'Abaqah* 22. The English translation of *'Abaqah* made by the present author is under print. Naṣīr Alī Sirhandī :

مرا بر صورت خويش آفريدى برون از خويشتن آخر چه ديدى

sarily mean the subtle speculations the philosophers are indulged in, nor what is peculiar to the mysteries, namely, the deep intuition, but the ones by which the men of sound constitution can find guidance in their livelihood and in their sciences which they gain from the side of their *Nasmah.* It is a science manifold and condensed which brings pleasure and satisfaction to the mind. It is not simply the impressions of the theoretical pictures in the mind nor does it mean the creation of the remote possibilities and the subtleties of no avail.[21]

Shāh Walīyullāh had profound knowledge of philosophy, and he justly claims to be the seal of philosophers and their place of refuge.[22]

21. *Al-Budūr-ul-Bāzighah*, p. 40.
22. *Al-Khair-ul-Kathīr*, p. 62:

و بعد مضى الف و مأة من الهجرة مال رجل منهم الى هذا النوع (قرب الوجود) من الكمال ، فكان امام المتقين و عصام الحكماء و ترجى من الله ان يجعل خاتم الحكماء المعصومين و لعل دعوته قد أجيبت - - -

Chapter XI

MISCELLANEOUS

Imām Mahdī

THE Traditions pertaining to the appearance of Imām Mahdī are the following:

(1) One day, when the Holy Prophet saw some young men of Banū Hāshim, his eyes became tearful and his complexion changed. When he was asked about the reason of that, he replied: "For us, God has preferred the future life to the present one. After my death, they will face many difficulties and will be driven away from their homeland. The descendants of my family will continue in this state until some people will come from the east, with black banners in their hands. They will ask for justice which will be denied to them. Then they will fight and would be victorious, and would get what they were asking for. They will then pass on all those things which they possessed to a descendant of my family, who will fill the earth with as much justice as it was filled with injustice before. Whosoever from you were to find himself alive at that time should present himself before him.[1]

(2) Three sons of a caliph will come to fight with each other for some treasure, but none of them will

1. Ibn Mājah, *Bāb Khurūj-ul-Mahdi*.

have it. After that people with black banners coming from the east will kill all of you. When you see them, lose no time in making an oath of allegiance to him (their leader), even though you may be made to suffer many a hardship in this way, because he would be the caliph Mahdī of God.[2]

(3) Once the Holy Prophet said that some people will come out from the east to pave the ground for Mahdī.[3]

Shāh Walīyullāh, while discussing the above-mentioned Traditions, is of opinion that by Mahdī here is meant the 'Abbāsī Caliph Mahdī and not the Promised Mahdī presumed to appear by the end of the life of this world. By the mention of Mahdī in the Tradition and his being called the caliph of God, and the encouragement given to people to support him was meant that caliphate had been destined for the Abbasids and this certainly was to come to pass. The intention here was the disclosure of the fact that, though many other aspirants to caliphate failed to achieve it, the Abbasids, however, will not fail, and their Mahdī is the caliph of God in the sense that the caliphate had been preordained for the Abbasids which they were to enjoy anyhow. The basically important thing in the *Sharī'ah* is that there should be order, peace and political stability in the country, and no disorder and disturbance anywhere, even though its ruler may not be possessed of all the requisite

2. Ibid.

3. Ibid.

qualifications.[4]

Another Tradition in this connection is that the Holy Prophet had said that if there would remain only one day in the life of the world, even then God would so prolong that day that someone from his family would come forth; he would be his namesake, his father's name would be like his father's name and he would establish order and justice in the world.[5]

This Tradition which has been mentioned in the *Sunan* of Abū Dāwūd also points out, says Shāh Ṣāḥib, to the caliph Mahdī of Banū Hāshim, because his name was Muhammad, his father's name was 'Abdullāh and he also descended from Banū Hāshim, the family of the Holy Prophet.

There are, however, certain Traditions reliable from the point of narration (*sanad*), referring to the Promised Mahdī and his appearance a little before the Judgment Day, but there seems to be no sense in our anxiously waiting for him, and having a belief that he would come one day, remove all the corruption and fill the earth with justice. One should continue one's struggle in one's life and make it (life) strong and prosperous from every point of view.

In this connection Shāh Ṣāḥib has referred to a revelation made to him: "Very soon the truth will be revealed to you which will break the old order of the

4. *Izālat-ul-Khafā'*, Vol. II, p. 157:

- - - و خلافت مستقره بهتر است اگرچه صاحب آن "کورک علی ضلع" باشد از خلافت متلاشیه گو صاحب آن افضل بود -

5. *Sunan Abū Dāwūd, Kitāb-ul-Mahdī.*

world. Signs of truth will shine on you to an extent that there would be no need of Mahdī any more and his appearance will be delayed for a long time."[6]

Besides, he has made a mention of Mahdī along with the advent of the Antichrist and the Prophet Jesus, from which it has become clear that he believed in the coming of Mahdī who would, however, appear at the approach of the Judgment Day.[7]

Superiority of the First Two Caliphs

The first two Caliphs have surpassed the other caliphs in their merits, because the service which they rendered to Islam was much greater than the service rendered by others. The period of their reign was remarkably distinguished by the rule of order and peace, and the establishment of political stability in the country. They indeed stand unrivalled in the efforts they made in strengthening, propagating and enforcing the commandments of the new faith.[8]

Explaining further Shāh Ṣāḥib says: Prophecy has twofold purpose to serve. One is the reception of knowledge direct from God, and the other isitsadequate publicity and dissemination among people. Now so far as the first purpose is concerned (namely, to receive knowledge from God), it is the sole right of the Holy Prophet himself and none else has a share therein;

6. *Tafhimāt*, Vol. II, pp. 120, 133.
7. *Al-Khair-ul-Kathīr*, pp. 112-13; *Izālat-ul-Khafā'*, Vol. I, p. 6:
... و همچنین بیقین میدانیم که شارع علیه الصلاة والسلام نص فرموده است بآنک امام مهدی در دامان قیامت موجود خواهد شد -
8. *Qurrat-ul-'Ainain*, pp. 136, 162, 209.

while so far as the other is related, this can be achieved only through the maintenance of law and order in the community, and there is absolutely no doubt that these qualities were comparatively found in abundance in the person of Abū Bakr and 'Umar, both during the life of the Holy Prophet and after his death. They brought unity and harmony among the Muslims and were well aware of the art of warfare.[9]

What the *Sharī'ah* requires is that its plain (*ẓāhir*) injunctions be acted upon, its orders be executed, and the people be made to obey them, and that there should be unity and peace among them. So far as the inner aspect (*bāṭin*) of the *Sharī'ah* is concerned which relates to the divine mysteries, self-annihilation, etc., it is itself dependent upon its outward aspect.[10]

By superiority is not meant that the first two Caliphs were superior to Ḥaḍrat 'Alī in relationship, intrepidity, strength and gnosis The reason of their pre-eminence is that through them Islam has benefited the most; and this is what determines superiority.[11]

In short, where the mystical sciences are concerned, 'Alī is superior to all, and this is why Ṣūfīs and mystics have reckoned him as such.[12]

Shāh Ṣāḥib was personally inclined towards 'Alī's superiority but he in his ecstatic contemplation of

9. *Ḥujjatullāh*, Vol. II, p. 215 ; *Ḥusn-ul-'Aqīdah*.

10. *Ad-Durr-uth-Thamīn fī Mubashsharāt-in-Nabiyy-il-Amīn*.

11. *Tafhīmāt*, Vol. I, p. 148 ; Vol. II, p. 172 ; *al-Khair-ul-Kathīr*, p. 90.

12. *Fuyūḍ-ul-Ḥaramain*, Mashhad, 22 ; *ad-Durr-uth-Thamīn fī Mubashsharāt-in-Nabiyy-il-Amīn*.

God, was advised not to come under the influence of that inclination; and he then followed that advice in right earnest.[13]

The most important point to take note of here is that the people should not abuse the Caliphs and should have no ill-talk against them. It is so, because, if the door of impugning is allowed to remain ajar, the chain of narration reaching the Holy Prophet would be cut off, and this in turn would become the cause of disunity and separation of the community.[14]

The Twelve Caliphs

The Traditions in connection with the twelve Caliphs are as under:

(1) Islam will continue in its true form and shape until the rule of twelve Caliphs over you, all of whom would be from the Quraish.

(2) The domination of Islam will continue until the rule of the twelve Caliphs, who without exception would be from the Quraish.

(3) The life of the people will always go on undisturbed until the twelve Caliphs have ruled over you, and that they all will be from the Quraish.[15]

Shāh Walīyullāh is of opinion that by those twelve Caliphs is meant the four Orthodox Caliphs, Mu'āwiyah, 'Abd-ul-Malik, his four sons and 'Abd-ul-'Azīz and Walīd b. 'Abd-ul-Malik.[16]

Explaining the above-mentioned Traditions he

13 *Fuyūḍ-ul-Ḥaramain*, Mashhad, 33.
14. *Waṣiyat Nāmah.*
15. *Ṣaḥīḥ Bukhārī.*
16. *Qurrat-ul-'Ainain*, pp. 296-97

observes that the common thing found in between the two governments, namely, of the Orthodox Caliphs and of the Umayyads, is that the domination of Islam has two aspects : one is the caliphate (rulership) and the other is the Holy Prophet's knowledge. Both the governments in relation to the caliphate were of the same type in the sense that in both of them the caliph ruled independently, and was free to act without the interference of the rebels, and without relying upon his army chiefs. This, however, was not the case during the Abbasid rule. Again, in both the governments there was a resemblance in respect of the religious science, because during the period of their reign, the different schools of thought had not been established as yet. No one was publicly saying that he was the follower of such and such religious leader. The jurisprudence of those times was replete with the works of Companions and their immediate Followers, and the people used to act upon all the Traditions, the *Mursal* as well as the *Musnad*.[17]

However, according to Shāh Ṣāḥib, by the Traditions as mentioned above in reference to the twelve Caliphs is not meant the twelve *Imāms* of the Shī'ites, as they never ruled as caliphs. In this connection he makes a mention of his ecstatic contemplation (*Mukāshafah*) as follows:

"I saw the spirits (*Arwāḥ*) of the *Imāms* of the Holy Prophet's family in the 'Holy Fold' (*Ḥaẓīrat-ul-Quds*) in an extremely beautiful and lovely shape and I was

17. *Izālat-ul-Khafā'*, Vol. I, pp. 155-56.

convinced that he who rejected and hated them was in great danger; but there, I found their faces turned towards the inward of the *Shari'ah*" while the caliphate can be acquired by one whose face is turned towards its outward. This is the reason why they sought caliphate but failed to acquire it.[18]

Splitting of the Moon

One of the miracles of the Holy Prophet is reported to have been the splitting of the moon. Shāh Sāhib at one place does not count it as his miracle and reckons it as one of the signs of the approach of Resurrection, when the moon will be split up. A reference towards it in the Holy Qur'ān is: "The resurrection has drawn nigh and the moon is split up." But because the Holy Prophet gave the news of the splitting of the moon in advance, therefore, in this respect it was his miracle. This, however, is the view of some eminent traditionists.[19]

In support of this view of his, he says, that it is not necessary that the moon must have been actually split up. Sometimes with the spread of dust in the sky, the breaking and falling of the stars, through the lunar and solar eclipses and some such other phenomenon in Nature, the moon might have appeared as split up. This, he says, is a possible case, but God is All-Powerful.[20]

However, Shāh Ṣāḥib in his poem which he com-

18. *Tafhimāt*, Vol. I, p. 107.

19. Ibid., Vol. II, p. 57; *Ta'wil-ul-Aḥādith*, pp. 81-82. Sūrah al-Qamar, verse 1.

20. *Ta'wil-ul-Aḥādith*, pp. 81-82.

posed in praise of the Holy Prophet, has recognised the "split of moon" as his miracle.[21]

This seemingly outward contradiction which is sometimes seen in the writings of Shāh Walīyullāh and which he himself acknowledges disappears when the matter in question is seriously considered from all aspects.

21. *Aṭyab-un-Nagham*, p. 15.

Chapter XII

THE LAST WORD

SOME contradiction is noticed at certain places in the writings of Shāh Walīyullāh which he himself frankly confesses, but he considers it as a result of his all-embracing nature, and this contradiction is not inner; it appears only outwardly.[1]

In our opinion, the way in which Shāh Ṣāḥib has presented the Islamic teachings before us is the right way. He says at one place that if people were to think seriously over the explanation of the Law (*Sharī'ah*) as given by him, they will find it in conformity with reason, tradition and intuition.[2]

The fact is that the prevalent conditions play an important role in the renovation and interpretation of the *Sharī'ah.* For example, if they demand its explanation by means of reason and philosophy, it is to be explained accordingly.[3]

In spite of that, we are not of those who, in order to encourage and propagate his teachings, want to thrust them upon people against their will, and for that, unhesitatingly, take such steps as become the

1 *Fuyūḍ-ul-Ḥaramain*, Mashhad, 33.

2. *Tafhimāt*, Vol. I, p 83 :

- - و كان كلامه بحيث ينطبق على البرهان والوجدان والمنقول -

3. Ibid., Vol. I, pp. 82-83:

- - و اذا كان الشائع فيهم البرهان و جب فى جوداللہ أن يكون تاويل الشريعة و تفسيرها بلسان البرهان - - -

cause of disruption of the Muslim community.

This attitude, however sincere it may be, is totally against the teachings of Shāh Walīyullāh. He worked for unity and discipline among the Muslims. Consequently, an action which implies the least possibility of division of the community is condemned by him.[4]

Such people can adequately benefit from his teachings who by their nature are inclined to research, provided it does not lead to any difference and conflict among the Muslims. It is, therefore, the duty of those who really wish to follow the path Shāh Walīyullāh had chosen, both in mysticism and jurisprudence, to refrain from every kind of such a move which may admit the possibility of their mutual clash and rivalry.[5]

The most outstanding quality, conspicuous everywhere in his writings, is his unemotionalism and the total absence of prejudice. He never writes anything under the impulse of emotion and nowhere exceeds the limits of justice and equity. From his writings it appears that whatever he is telling had already come under his personal experience, supported by his veridical vision.[6]

Shāh Sāhib was undoubtedly an *Imām* of his age. His works on different topics, whether these topics treated were political, economic, social, cultural, historical or philosophical and religious, unmistakably bear the stamp of his originality and creativity.

He had complete command over the Arabic

4. *Fuyūḍ-ul-Ḥaramain*, Mashhad, 31.

5. Ibid., 10.

6 *Tafhimāt*, Vol. I, p. 83.

language, and this is the reason that he produced many valuable works on various subjects with ease and thoroughness. He knew both Arabic and Persian poetry, but in spite of that he cannot be called a poet. While writing poetry he selected *Amīn* as his *nom-de-plume*, and this was probably because of his close attachment with his colleague Shaikh Muḥammad Amīn Kashmīrī.[7]

7. *Al-Faḍl-ul-Mubīn fi'l-Musalsal min Ḥadīth-i*-*Nabiyy-il-Amīn*.

BIBLIOGRAPHY

(1) *Works by Shāh Walīyullāh*

1. *Fa'h-ur-Raḥmān* (P)*
2. *Fatḥ-ul-Khabīr* (A)
3. *Al-Fauz-ul-Kabīr fī Uṣūl-it-Tafsr* (P)
4. *Muqaddimah dar Fann-i-Tarjimah-i-Qur'ān* (P)
5. *Al-Muqaddimah fī Qawānīn Tarjimah* (P)
6. *Ḥujjatullāh-ul-Bālighah* (A)
7. *Al-Budūr-ul-Bāzighah* (A)
8. *Al-Khair-ul-Kathīr* (A)
9. *Al-Tafhīmāt-ul-Ilāhīyyah* (A) (P)
10. *Fuyūḍ-ul-Ḥaramain* (A)
11. *Al-Muṣaffā* (P)
12. *Al-Musawwā* (A)
13. *An-Nawādir min Aḥādīth Sayyid-il-Awā'il wa'l-Awākhir* (A)
14. *Al-Faḍl-ul-Mubīn fi'l-Musalsal min Ḥadīth-in-Nabīyyil-Amīn* (A)
15. *'Arba'ūna Ḥadīthan Musalsalatan bi'l-Ishrāf fī Ghālib Sanadihā* (A)
16. *Ad-Durr-uth-Thamīn fī Mubashsharāt-in-Nabīyy-il-Amīn* (A)
17. *Surūr-ul-Maḥzūn* (Persian translation of *Kitāb Nur-ul-'Uyūn* by Ibn Sayyid-in-Nās)
18. *Al-Irshād ilā Muhimmāt 'Ilm-ıl-Isnād* (A)
19. *Tarājim-ul-Bukhārī* (A)

* (A) and (P) appearing after the names of books indicate Arabic and Persian.

20. *Sharḥ Tarājim Ba'ḍ Abwāb-il-Bukhārī* (A)
21. *Inṣāf fī Bayān Sabab-il-Ikhtilāf* (A)
22. *'Iqd-ul-Jīd fī Aḥkām-il-Ijtihād wa't-Taqlīd* (A)
23. *Izālat-ul-Khafā' 'an Khilāfat-il-Khulafā'* (P)
24. *Qurrat-ul-'Ainain fī Tafḍīl-ish-Shaikhain* (P)
25. *Al-Qaul-ul-Jamīl* (A)
26. *Hama'āt* (P)
27. *Saṭa'āt* (P)
28. *Lamaḥāt* (A)
29. *Alṭāf-ul-Quds* (P)
30. *Ta'wīl-ul-Aḥādīth* (A)
31. *Intibāh fī Salāsil Auliyā' Allāh* (P)
32. *Intibāh fī Salāsil Auliyā Allāh wa Asānīd Wārithi Rasūlillāh* (P)
33. *As-Sirr-ul-Maktūm fī Asbāb Tadwīn-il-'Ulūm* (A)
34. *Maktūbāt Ma'hū Manāqib Abī 'Abdullāh Muḥammad b. Ismā'īl al-Bukhārī wa Faḍīlat Ibn taimīyyah* (P)
35. *Maktūb-i-Madanī* (A)
36. *Maktūb-ul-Ma'ārif ma'Ḍamīmah Maktūb Thalāthah* (P)
37. *Kalimāt-i-Ṭayyibāt* (*Maktūbāt*) (P)
38. *Maktūbāt* (contained in *Ḥayāt-i-Walī*) (A)
39. *Maktūbāt* (contained in *Walīyullāh Dehlawī Key Siyāsī Maktūbāt*) (P)
40. *Anfās-ul-'Ārifīn* (P)
41. *Imdād fī Ma'athir-il-Ajdād* (P)
42. *'Aṭiyat-uṣ-Ṣamadīyyah fi'l-Anfās-il-Muḥammadīyyah* (P)
43. *Insān-ul-'Ain fī Mashā'ikh-il-Ḥaramain* (P)
44. *Hawāmi'* (*Sharḥ-i-Ḥizb-ul-Baḥr*) (P)
45. *Al-Juz'-ul-Laṭīf* (P)

46. *Waṣīyat Nāmah* (P)
47. *Ḥusn-ul-'Aqīdah* (A)
48. *Risālah-i-Dānishmandī* (P)
49. *Kashf-ul-Ghain fī Sharḥ-i'r-Rubā'iyatain* (P)
50. *Aṭyab-un-Naghm fī Madḥ Sayyīd-i'l-'Arab wa'l-'Ajam* (A)
51. *Ṣarf-i-Mīr* (P)

(2) *Works by Shāh Walīyullāh's Descendants and His Father*

1. *Fatḥ-ul-'Azīz*
2. *Fatāwā-i-'Azīzī*
3. *Fī Mā Yajib Ḥifẓuhū li'n-Nāẓir*
4. *'Ujjālah Nāfi'ah*
5. *Malfūẓāt*

(1–5) } *by Shāh 'Abd-ul-'Azīz*

6. *Anfās-i-Raḥīmīyah* by Shāh 'Abd-ur-Rahīm
7. *Irshād-i-Raḥīmīyah* by Shāh 'Abd-ur-Rahīm
8. *'Abaqāt* by Shāh Ismā'īl Shahīd
9. *Taqwiyat-ul-Īmān* by Shāh Ismā'īl Shahīd
10. *Mūḍiḥ-i-Qur'ān* by Shāh 'Abd-ul-Qādir

(3) *Works by Maulānā 'Ubaidullāh Sindhī*

1. *Ilhām-ur-Raḥmān fī Tafsīr il-Qur'ān*
2. *Al-Maqām-ul-Maḥmūd*
3. *Qur'ān Karīm kā Muqaddimah aur Sūrah Fātiaḥahī kī Tafsīr*
4. *Qur'ān Pāk kā Muṭāli'ah Kaisey Kīyā Jāey*
5. *Tamad un-i-'Arab*, Tafsīr Sūrah Sabā'
6. *Risālatun fī Muṣṭaliḥ-il-Ḥadīth wa Sharḥ Ba'ḍ 'Ibārāt-in-Nukhbah*

7. *Shāh Walīyullāh aur Un kā Falsafah*
8. *Shāh Walīyullāh aur Un kī Siyāsī Taḥrīk*
9. *Qu'rānī Dastūr-i-Inqilāb*
10. *'Unwān-i-Inqilāb*
11. *Risālah-i-Maḥmūdīyah*
12. *Dhātī Diary*
13. *Urdū Sharḥ Ḥujjatullāh-ul-Bālighah*

(4) *Miscellaneous*

1. *Maulānā 'Ubaidullāh Sindhī, Ḥālāt-i-Zindagī, Ta'līmāt, aur Siyāsī Afkār* by Professor Muḥammad Sarwar
2. *Taṣawwuf kī Ḥaqīqat aur Us Kā Falsafah-i-Ta'rīkh* (Urdu translation of *Hama'āt*) by Professor Muḥammad Sarwar
3. *Mushāhidāt wa Ma'ārif* (Urdu translation of *Fuyūḍ-ul-Ḥaramain*) by Professor Muḥammad Sarwar
4. *Maulānā 'Ubaidullāh Sindhī aur Un key Nāqid* by Maulānā Sa'īd Aḥmad Akbarābādī
5. *Tadhkirah Shāh Walīyullah* by 'Allāmah Manāẓir Aḥsan Gīlānī
6. *Shāh Walīyullāh key 'Umrānī Naẓriye* by Shams-ur-Raḥmān Muḥsinī
7. *Shāh Walīyullāh aur Un kā Falsafah-i-'Umrānīyāt wa Ma'āshīyāt* by Shaikh Bashīr Aḥmad Ludhianawi, B.A.
8. *Ifādāt-i-Ḥaḍrat Shāh Walīyullāh Dihlawī* by Ṣadr-ud-Dīn Iṣlāḥī
9. *Rūd-i-Kauthar* by Shaikh Muḥammad Ikrām, M.A., I.C.S.

10. *Tadhkirah 'Ulamā'-i-Hind* by Rahmān 'Alī
11. *Al-Furqān*, Bareili, 1941 (Shāh Walīyullāh Number) by Maulānā Raḥīm Bakhsh Dihlawī
12. *Ḥayāt-i-Walī* by Maulānā Raḥīm Bakhsh Dihlawī
13. *Al-Kalām* by 'Allāmah Shiblī
14. *Nuzhat-ul-Khawāṭir wa Bahjat-ul-Masāmi' wa'n-Nawāẓir* by 'Abd-ul-Ḥayy al-Ḥasanī
15. *Ath-Thaqāfat-ul-Islāmīyah fī'l-Hind* by 'Abd-ul-Ḥayy al-Ḥasanī
16. *Al-Yāni'-ul-Janīy fi'l-Asānīd Shaikh 'Abd-ul-Ghanī* by Muḥsin b. Yaḥyā at-Turhatī
17. *Sharḥ Ḥadīth Abī Razīn* by Maulānā Muḥammad Qāsim Nānotawī
18. *Ethical Philosophy of Shāh Walīyullāh* by Dr. A.J. Halepota, University of Sind
19. *Islamic Culture*, October 1947 issue and July and October 1962 issues, Hyderabad Deccan
20. *The Mujaddid's Conception of Tawḥīd* by Dr. Burhān Aḥmad Fārūqī, Aligarh Muslim University
21. *The Contribution of India to Arabic Literature* by Dr. Zubaid Aḥmad
22. *India's Contribution to the Study of Ḥadīth Literature* by Dr. Muḥammad Isḥāq, University of Dacca
23. "Two Lists of Prophets: A Comparison between Ibn al-'Arabī's *Fuṣūṣ-ul-Ḥikam* and Shāh Walīyullāh al-Dihlawī's *Ta'wīl-ul-Aḥadīth*". (A paper read by Dr J.M.S. Baljon at the III congresso di studi Arabi e Islamici, Ravello, 1-6 September 1966).
24. J.M.S. Baljon, "Psychology As Apprehended and

Applied by Shāh Walīyullāh Dihlawi," *Proceedings of the Congress of the Dutch Oriental Society*, held in Leiden on 8-9 May 1970.